MY SPACE BOOK

Danielle Robichaud

THE SECRETS OF THE UNIVERSE

We live on a planet, which on a human scale, can appear to be quite big. However, the Earth is nothing but a small point in a very large universe.

Thousands of scientists of all disciplines continue their work to uncover the deepest mysteries of the universe.

CONTENTS

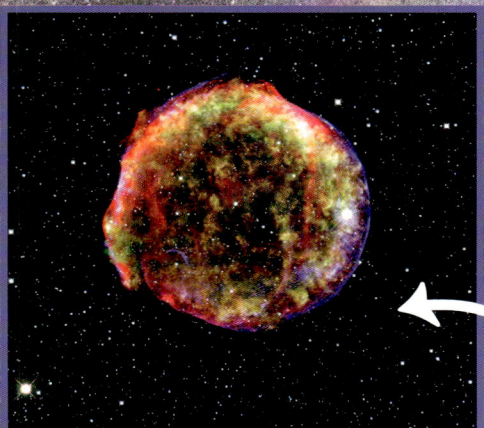

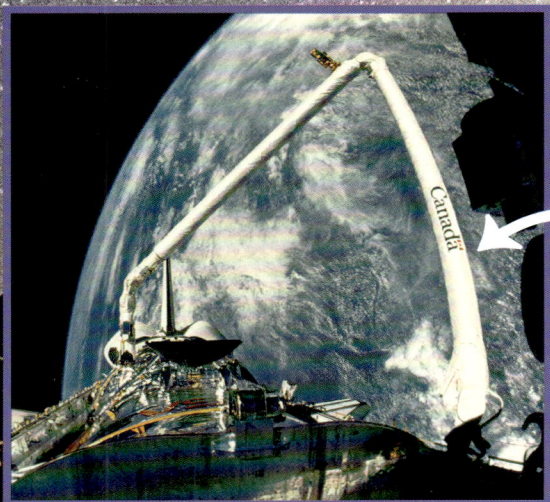

THE GREAT ASTRONOMERS

For thousands of years, humans have been observing the skies and have used their knowledge of them to navigate and even to predict the future. One of the most well-known ideas that spread across cultures was that Earth was flat and that the universe, including its stars and its Sun made up the sky over our heads.

However, in the age of the Antiquities, Pythagoras of Samos, a Greek philosopher and mathematician began with an idea that the Earth was round. From then on, in the 2nd century, Eratosthenes calculated the circumference of the Earth in a very precise manner by observing the position of the Sun during the summer solstice.

For more than 1,000 years, the catholic church upheld the idea that the Earth was immobile and was the center of the universe, a theory called geocentrism. This belief was anchored in the Christian faith and it became very dangerous to contest it.

NICOLAUS COPERNICUS

(1473-1543)

The idea that the Sun is the center of the universe and that the planets and the Earth gravitate around the star was proposed by Nicolaus Copernicus. This Polish astronomer developed the heliocentric theory that places the Sun at the center of our solar system.

Copernicus knew that this theory would not garner unanimity among the scholars of the church. This is why he had his discoveries published after his death.

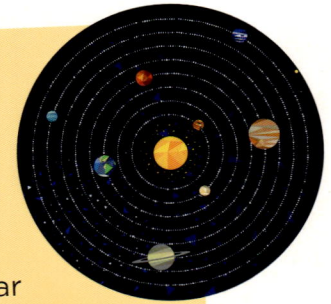

GALILEO

(1564-1642)

The Italian mathematician and astronomer Galileo was the first man to have observed the sky with an astronomical telescope. He was able to show that the Milky Way was made up of stars, invisible to the naked eye, that around Jupiter, there were four satellites and that the Moon had craters. At the end of his life, Galileo was imprisoned by the church for having tried to prove Copernicus's theory that the Earth and the planets circled the Sun. During his trial, he officially renounced his convictions to avoid the death penalty.

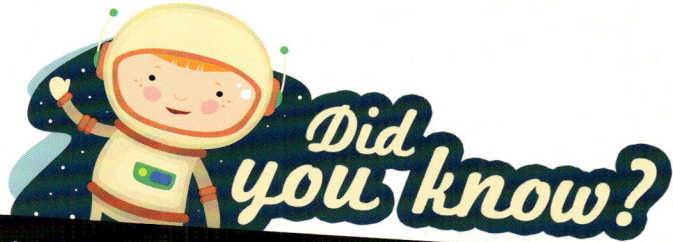

ISAAC NEWTON

(1642-1727)

We owe several scientific theories to Isaac Newton, one of which was universal gravitation. This theory explains that all bodies attract one another. The higher their mass, the higher the attractive force. Newton's laws helped to predict the movements of the planets as well as motion and attraction of objects in the entire universe. For example, when an object falls, the force of gravity imparted on it by the Earth attracts it towards the ground. The same object would float if it wasn't subjected to this force.

EDWIN HUBBLE

(1889-1953)

The American astronomer spent his life in the most important observatories in the world.

Thanks to his observations and calculations, he was able to show the existence of other galaxies during an era where people believed that the universe was strictly composed of our solar system. Hubble also showed that the universe was expanding. In many ways, he discovered the cosmos.

SPACE-BASED OBSERVATION

For ages, humans have had a deep curiosity for the skies and been in search of signs. The ancient civilizations attributed signs to the special movement of the stars. More than 7,000 years later, we still—to this day—avidly watch the skies. Our tools are more sophisticated and they allow us to see further than we could ever have into the universe.

Over 3,000 years ago, the scholars from the Babylonian empire in the Middle East began writing their observations of the skies on **clay tablets**.

Before the invention of the telescope, observations of the skies were made with the naked eye. The **octant** is an ancient navigational instrument that navigators used to calculate the position of the stars in the sky.

The **astrolabe** was an instrument that astronomers used to measure the height of celestial bodies. Navigators used it to tell time in relation to the position of the stars and the Sun.

The first telescopes were made by the Dutch in the 17th century. Basing himself on these models, Galileo made an **astronomer's telescope** that could enlarge objects dozen times its size.

TYCHO BRAHE

The astronomer Tycho Brahe had an **underground observatory** built on the Danish island Stjerneborg, which means "the palace of the stars." Over the course of several decades, he and his collaborators made a large number of observations. He is known to have observed the emergence of a super-nova and the trajectory of a comet. He is also well known for having developed measurement instruments for astronomy such as the armillary sphere that was used to more accurately measure the coordinates of the stars in order to understand their celestial movements.

It is due to **William Herschel's** (1738-1822) own handmade telescopes that the planet Uranus was discovered in 1781.

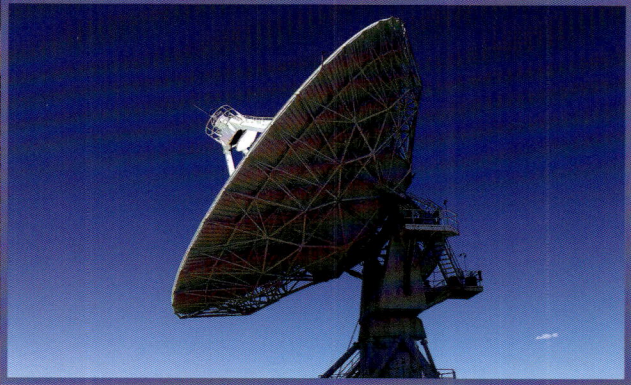

Observatories are usually built on the ground at the highest points of mountains, far from cities. They house giant telescopes, radio telescopes and other sophisticated photography instruments.

Space probes are used to collect information on certain objects in our solar system such as the Sun and the planets. Launched in 1964, the *Mariner 4* probe sent us the first images of the surface of Mars.

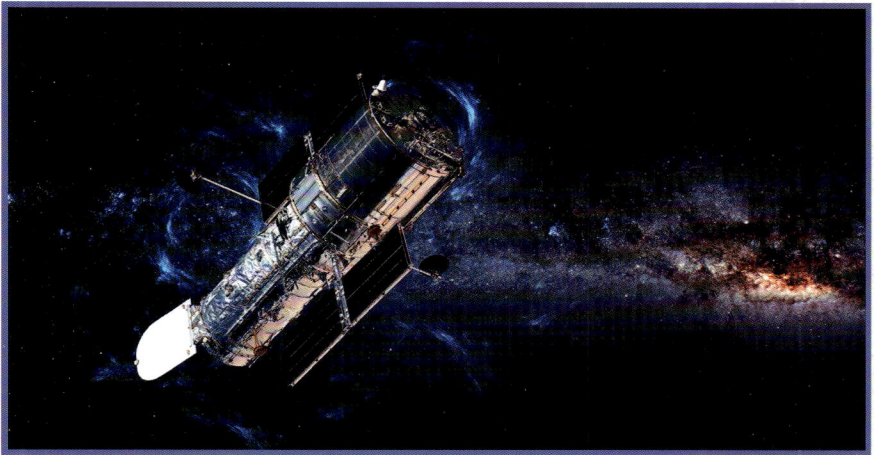

The *Hubble* **space telescope**, launched in 1990, captures the light that originates from very far in the universe. It measures 13 meters (42 feet) (the size of a bus) and gravitates around the Earth.

A new generation of telescopes will soon be in service thanks to NASA. The infrared telescope *James-Webb* will allow scientists to study the evolution of the universe. It will orbit around the Sun at a distance of 1.5 million kilometers (932,056 miles) from Earth.

THE EARTH

1 natural satellite: the Moon

The Earth is 4.6 billion years old! Since its creation, our planet has gone through several transformations. With time, its surface has cooled to form a solid crust.

Diameter: 12,000 km (7,456 mi.)

Orbital period: 365.25 terrestrial days

Average distance to the Sun: 150 million km (93 million mi.)

Surface temperature: between 58 and -89 °C (136 °F and -67 °F)

THE COMPOSITION

The Earth is the largest telluric planet. It is mainly composed of rocks and metals.

The **internal core** is very hot and partially solid. It is made up of iron and nickel.

The **external core** is made up of liquid metals.

The **mantle** makes up a major part of the terrestrial mass. This layer is somewhat solid.

The **Earth's crust**, also called lithosphere, is made up of solid rock.

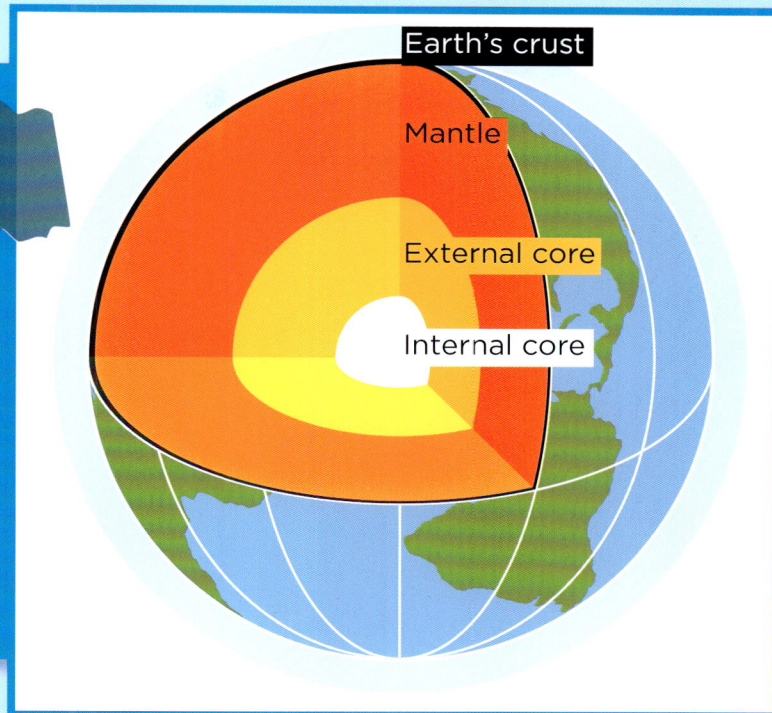

Earth's crust

Mantle

External core

Internal core

Did you know?

The first living beings that appeared on Earth 3.8 billion years ago were microscopic and unicellular microbes.

THE PANGAEA

450 million years ago, the 7 continents formed a single giant continent called Pangaea. For thousands of years, tectonic movements created fissures in Pangaea, forming separate continents.

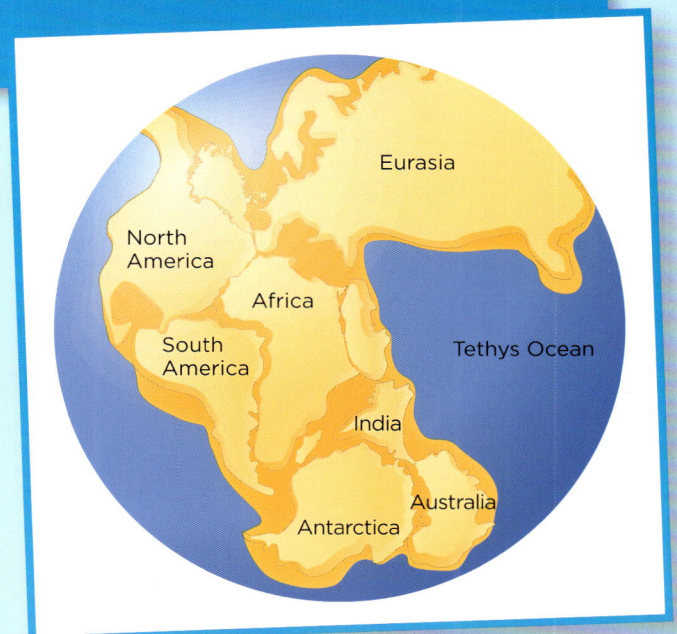

SHOOTING STARS

Sometimes debris from space penetrates into our atmosphere at high speeds. These small meteors are rapidly destroyed as they come into contact with the gases in our atmosphere, leaving a light trail that disappears in a few seconds. In reality, these shooting stars are not stars at all, but simply little pieces of comets.

During certain periods of the year, we can observe several shooting stars in the sky. These phenomena occur when the Earth crosses the orbit of an ancient comet. The debris left behind by the comet enters into our terrestrial atmsphere, giving us a spectacular view. The perseides, a shower of shooting stars, happens in the month of August every year.

Eurasia

North America

Africa

South America

Tethys Ocean

India

Australia

Antarctica

THE EARTH'S ATMOSPHERE

From outer space, the Earth looks like an immense blue sphere streaked in white. This is due to the fact that our planet is covered in water from rivers, glaciers and oceans, which makes up more than 75% of its surface.

The atmosphere, which is made up of a **mixture of gases**, surrounds the Earth and protects the millions of living species from the toxic rays of the Sun and from the debris in space. It is principally composed of **nitrogen** (78%) and **oxygen** (21%). Without **water** and the **atmosphere**, life would not be able to exist on our planet.

Meteorites

A hurricane

Lightning

THE EXOSPHERE
The exosphere is the limit between the Earth's atmosphere and space, where most of the satellites orbit.

THE THERMOSPHERE
The aurora borealis, spectacular phenomena caused by the friction of gas atoms and solar particles, occurs in the thermosphere.

THE MESOSPHERE
Located 50 km (31 mi.) above the Earth's surface, temperatures reach glacial levels in the mesosphere.

THE STRATOSPHERE
This is where the ozone layer is located. Ozone is a gas that protects Earth's organisms from the Sun's dangerous ultraviolet rays.

THE TROPOSPHERE
This layer is the densest and closest to Earth's surface. It makes up the air that we breathe! The troposphere is also where certain meteorological phenomena occur such as clouds, rain and lightning.

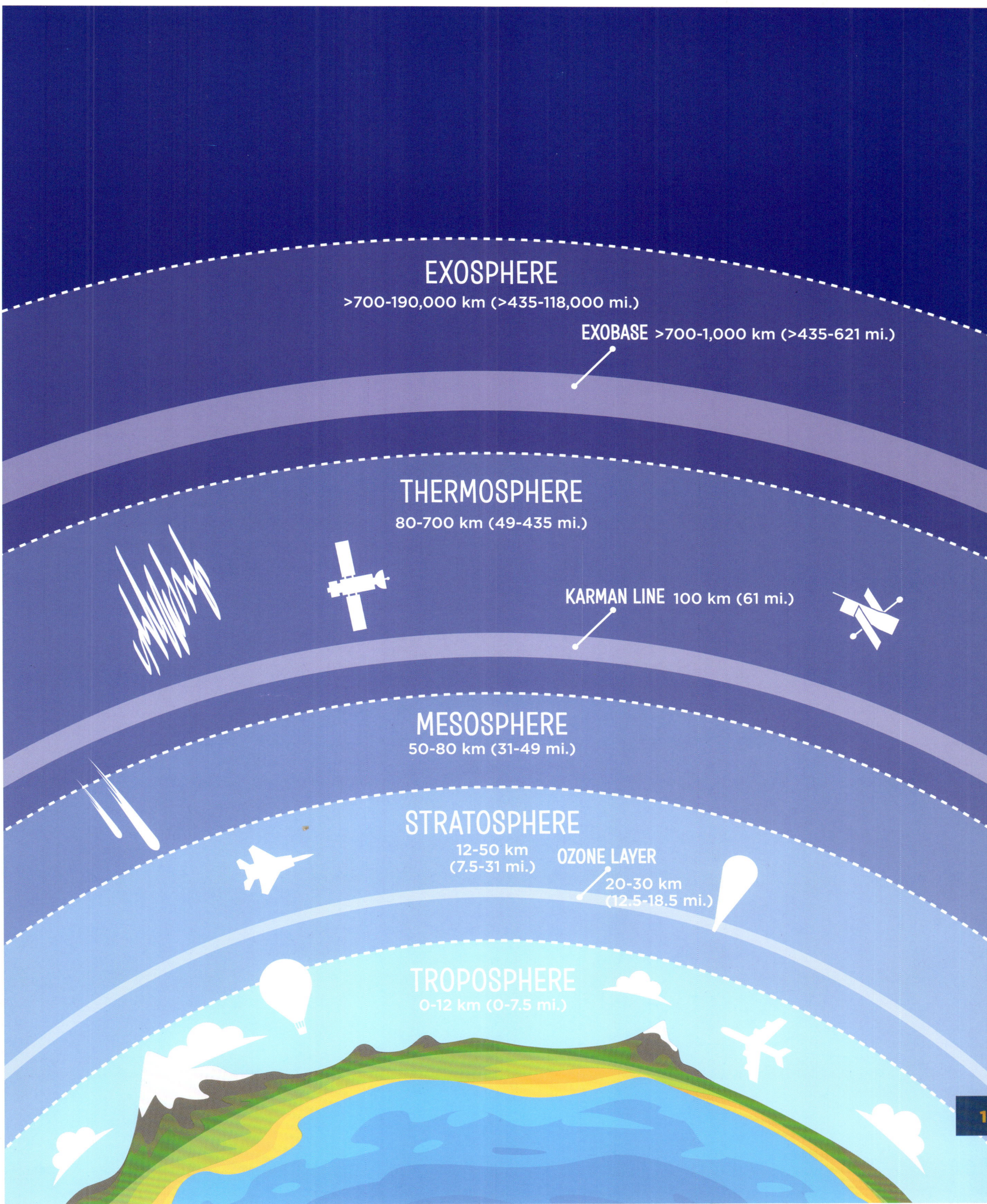

EXOSPHERE
>700-190,000 km (>435-118,000 mi.)

EXOBASE >700-1,000 km (>435-621 mi.)

THERMOSPHERE
80-700 km (49-435 mi.)

KARMAN LINE 100 km (61 mi.)

MESOSPHERE
50-80 km (31-49 mi.)

STRATOSPHERE
12-50 km
(7.5-31 mi.)

OZONE LAYER
20-30 km
(12.5-18.5 mi.)

TROPOSPHERE
0-12 km (0-7.5 mi.)

11

THE MAGNETIC FIELD AND THE AURORA BOREALIS

The movement of **liquid metal** in the external core of the Earth creates a **magnetic field** around the Earth. Earth acts as a giant magnet on solar particles.

The aurora borealis is films of color that dances in the northern night sky. This occurs when solar winds react with the Earth's magnetic field. This fascinating show can happen further south when eruptions occur on the surface of the Sun.

VOLCANOES

There are thousands of volcanoes on the **surface of the Earth**, but also at the **bottom of oceans**. Some are extinct, however others are still active. Small faults in the crust allows volcanoes to form. The **magma** that comes from the mantle escapes from these openings to form the solid structures, which are rather large.

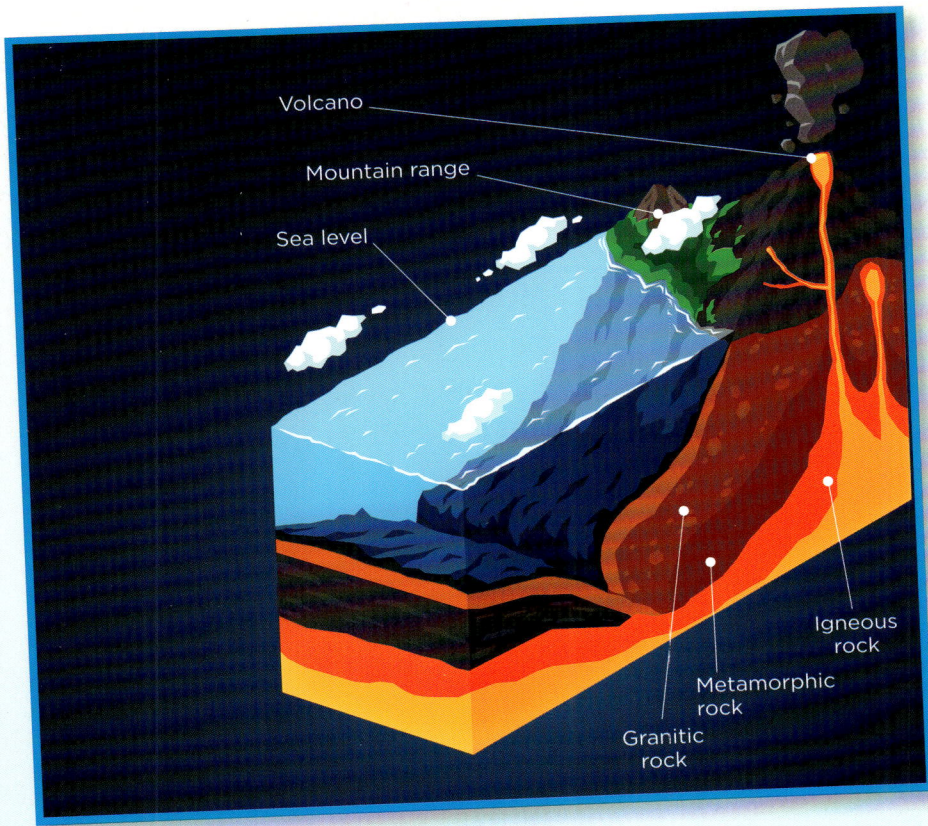

THE TECTONIC PLATES

The Earth's crust is formed from a thousand large, rocky plates called tectonic plates. These move constantly causing earthquakes, the formation of mountains and volcanic eruptions.

The movement of tectonic plates produce the landscapes that we see everywhere on Earth.

THE TIDES

Did you know that tides are caused by the **attractive forces of the Moon**? When the Moon orbits around our planet, it attracts the side of the Earth facing it.

The Sun also exerts an influence on the tides even if it is farther away. When the Moon and the Sun are aligned with Earth, they both produce strong tides called spring tides.

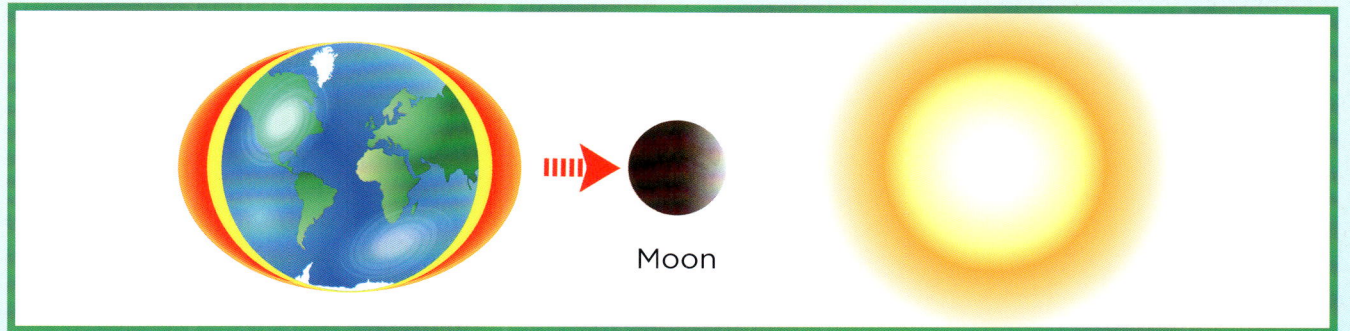

THE GREENHOUSE GAS EFFECT

The gases that surround Earth also heat it. This is what we call the greenhouse gas effect. The gas has a greenhouse effect that entraps the infrared rays of the Sun penetrating the atmosphere. They produce an effect similar to a greenhouse where the glass keeps in the heat. Without this phenomenon, it would be very cold and Earth would be frozen solid.

THE MOON

If the Moon appears to be shining, it is nothing but an illusion. In reality, it reflects the rays from the Sun like a giant mirror. It reflects approximately 7% of the Sun's rays back to us.

LUNAR CYCLES

Over the course of several weeks, the Moon changes its appearance in the night's sky. It appears round, like a plate. Other times it takes the shape of a crescent. **Lunar phases** are due to the fact that the Moon orbits around the Earth. Since the position relative to the Sun changes constantly, the Moon reflects the rays of light on a sometimes very large surface. A lunar cycle, in other words, the period that elapses between two new Moons, is 29.5 days.

LUNAR ECLIPSES

When the Moon is in the **shadow of the Earth**, there is a lunar eclipse. An eclipse can be either total or partial. The Moon appears to us as a red disk in the sky. Total eclipses can last several hours. Contrary to solar eclipses, lunar eclipses are not a danger to the eyes.

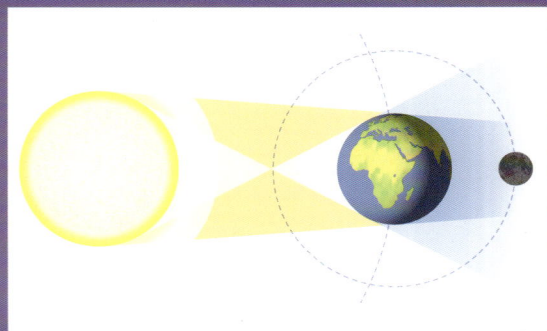

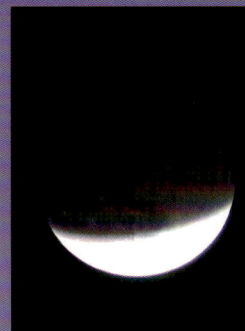

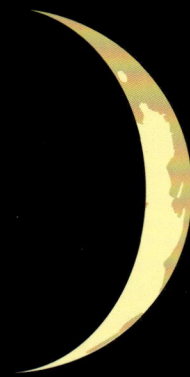

NEW MOON   FIRST CRESCENT   FIRST QUARTER   WAXING GIBBOUS CRESCENT

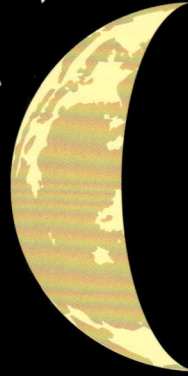

When the Moon is between the Earth and the Sun, it is almost invisible from Earth. This is the new Moon.

When a surface is composed of bumps, we called it Gibbous. The Moon is in its Gibbous phase when we can see more than half of its surface.

FULL MOON   WANING GIBBOUS CRESCENT   LAST QUARTER   LAST CRESCENT

When the Earth is between the Sun and the Moon, we may observe the entire surface of the Moon. This is the full Moon.

THE SOLAR SYSTEM

At the center of our solar system is a star, our Sun. This is the largest and most massive element in our solar system. The enormous gravitational force of the Sun maintains the equilibrium of the solar system. This is how the objects of the system gravitate around it.

All the planets rotate around themselves and revolve around the Sun. The trajectory that the planets follow is called an orbit. The orbit of planets is not perfectly round, but more elliptical. Dwarf planets, satellites, asteroids and comets also make up our solar system.

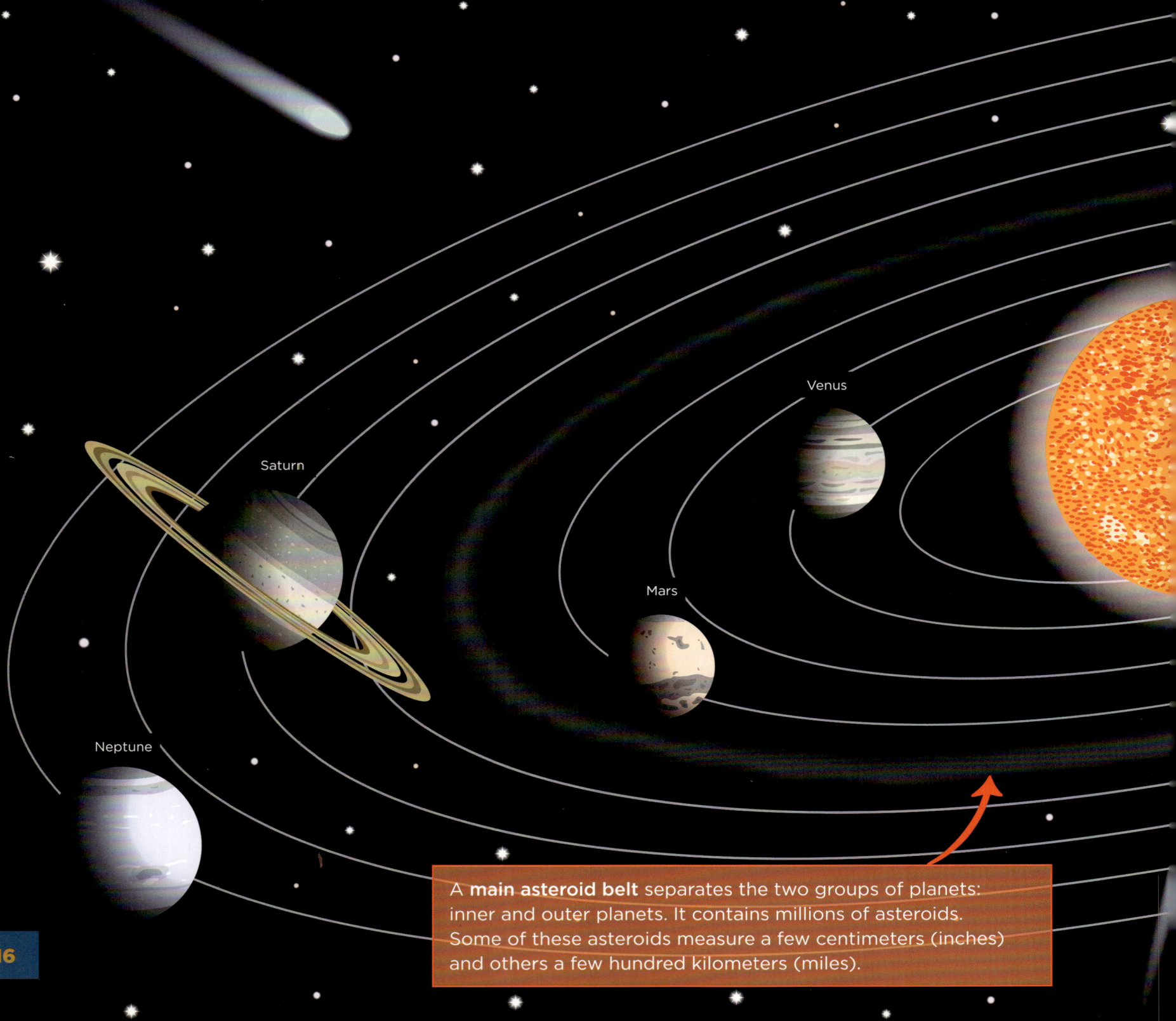

Venus

Saturn

Mars

Neptune

A **main asteroid belt** separates the two groups of planets: inner and outer planets. It contains millions of asteroids. Some of these asteroids measure a few centimeters (inches) and others a few hundred kilometers (miles).

Far away from the outer planets is the **Kuiper belt**. This is a flat expanse of asteroids that is 20 times larger than the main asteroid belt. Cosmic debris makes up the remainder of the solar system.

Jupiter

Mercury

Uranus

Earth

The Oort cloud surrounds our solar system like a shell. It is formed of inactive and frozen comets. It is located at the gravitational frontier of the Sun.

The solar system formed 4.6 billion years ago. When this happened, a great cloud of gas called the nebulous cloud contracted to form a new star, the Sun.

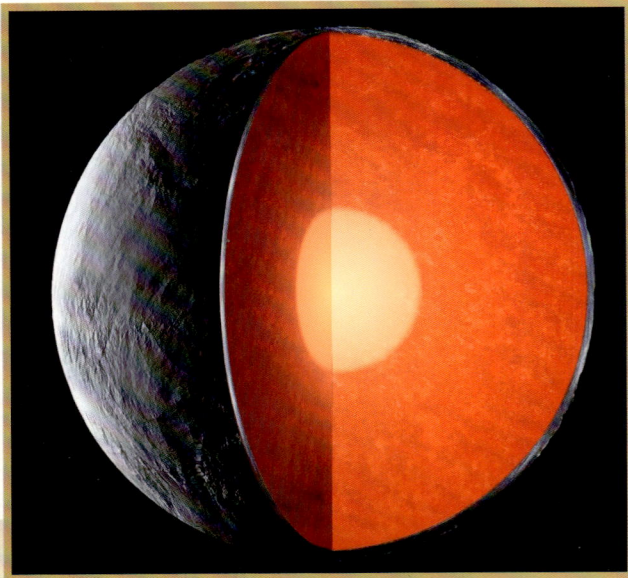

Mercury, Venus, Earth and Mars are the inner planets, also called **telluric** planets. These are rocky planets that contain an iron core.

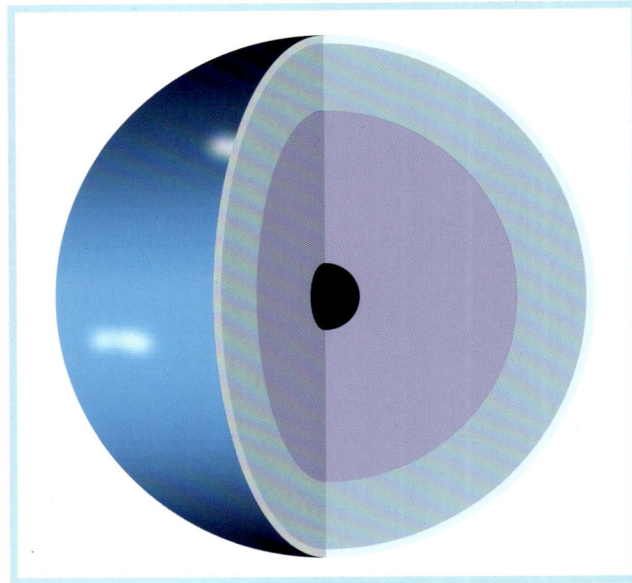

Jupiter, Saturn, Uranus and Neptune are the outer planets, also called the **gas giants**. These are the largest planets in our solar system. They are made up, in part, of a mixture of gases.

PLUTO AND THE DWARF PLANETS

Pluto was discovered in 1930. It was long considered a planet, however Pluto lost its status in 2006 after the International Astronomical Union created a new definition for what constituted a planet. We now consider Pluto to be a **dwarf planet**.

Four other objects in our solar system are classified as dwarf planets: Ceres, Haumea, Makemake and Eris. It is expected that other objects will also be incorporated into the list in the years to come.

NEW HORIZONS

In January 2006, NASA sent a probe called New Horizon toward Pluto. The probe took more than **9 years** to reach Pluto and its **Moon, Charron**. In 2015, New Horizon sent back the first close-up images of the surface of Pluto. The New Horizon probe continues its journey in the **Kuiper belt**. To this day, the probe has traveled up to **6.6 billion kilometers** (4.1 billion miles) from Earth.

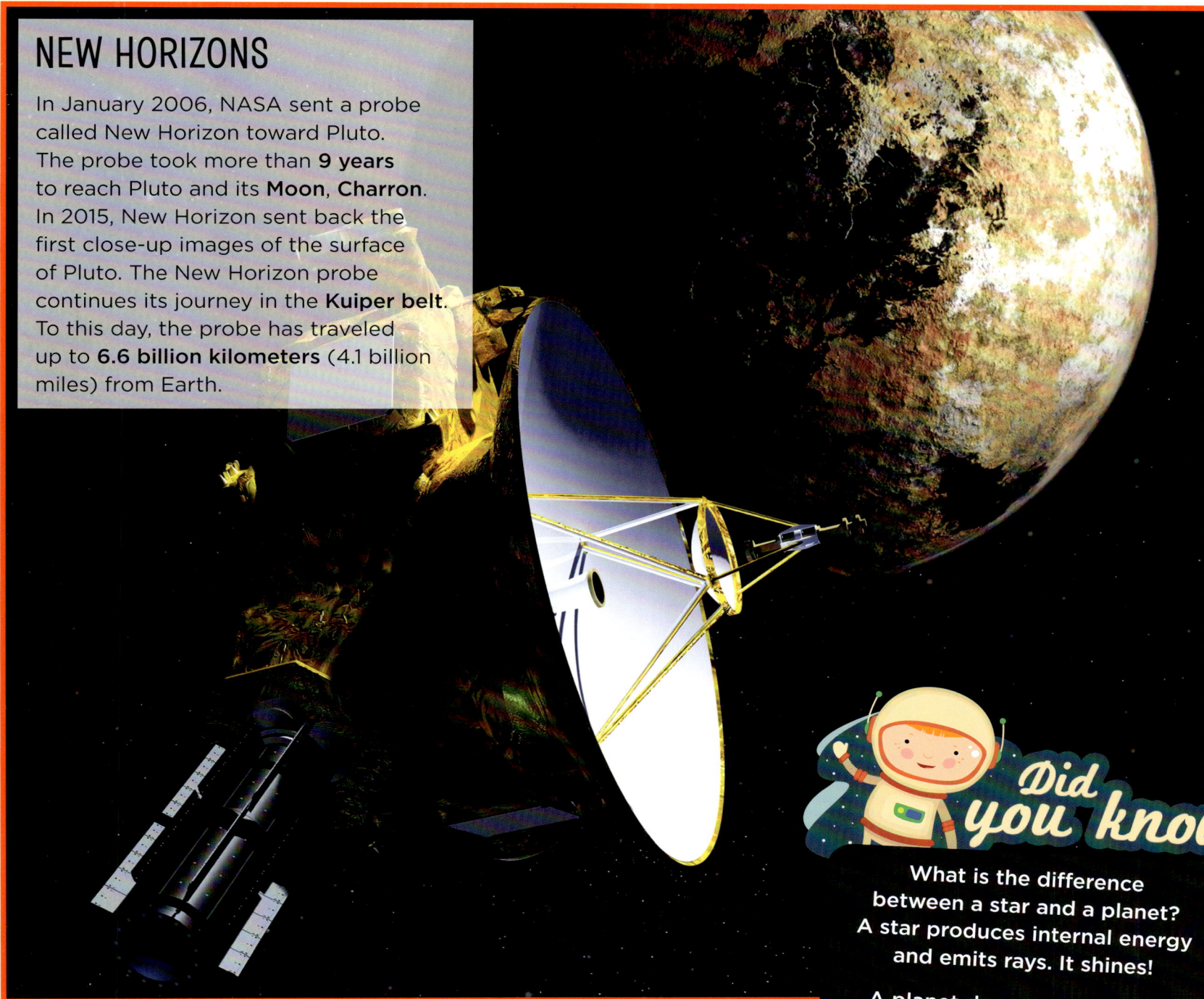

Did you know?

What is the difference between a star and a planet? A star produces internal energy and emits rays. It shines!

A planet does not emit light, it reflects light. It also orbits around a star.

COMETS

Comets are made of a mixture of **ice** and **rocky dust**. They come from far away in our solar system, from the Oort cloud. When they approach the Sun, comets release dust and ice at their surface which vaporize. This forms a long, bright tail that can be seen from Earth.

In 1696, Edmond Halley, who was the astronomer to the king of England predicted the passage of a comet in 1758. By doing research, he compared the observations of comets from 1531, 1607 and 1682. He concluded that the observed comets were one and the same comet. **Halley's Comet** is periodical, which means that it travels the same trajectory in a given interval of time. Hence, it can be observed every 76 years. The Comet's next visit will therefore be in the year 2062.

THE SUN

Our Sun is nothing but a star among billions that exist in our universe. However, the Sun is the closest to our planet.

WHAT IS THE SUN MADE OF?

The Sun is actually a giant **ball of gas** that has been burning for 4.6 billion years. It is about 110 times bigger than the size of Earth. If our planet were the size of a pea, the Sun would be the size of a tire!

The energy of the Sun comes from a chemical reaction that occurs at its center. This chemical phenomenon is called **fusion**. Fusion occurs when the particles combine to form new material. This reaction releases a large quantity of energy. The particles of light, called **photons**, travel very far into the universe.

THE SUN AND LIFE

Before life on Earth appeared, the Earth's atmosphere contained very little oxygen. The combination of solar energy, water vapor and carbon gas caused a chemical reaction. The first **microorganisms** started to produce **oxygen**. Over a period of 2 billion years, this phenomenon changed the entire composition of the atmosphere. Today, oxygen constitutes 21% of the air that we breathe.

The Mayan and Aztec civilizations built large temples in honor of the Sun. The Egyptians gave it the name Re and considered it to be a god. Louis XIV, the king of France, made the Sun his royal symbol. He was known as the Sun King.

A PROBE TOWARDS THE SUN

The *Parker* probe, which was launched in 2018, was sent with the intent of revolutionizing our understanding of the atmosphere and the Sun's crown. It was sent to give us raw information on the temperature and its radiation.

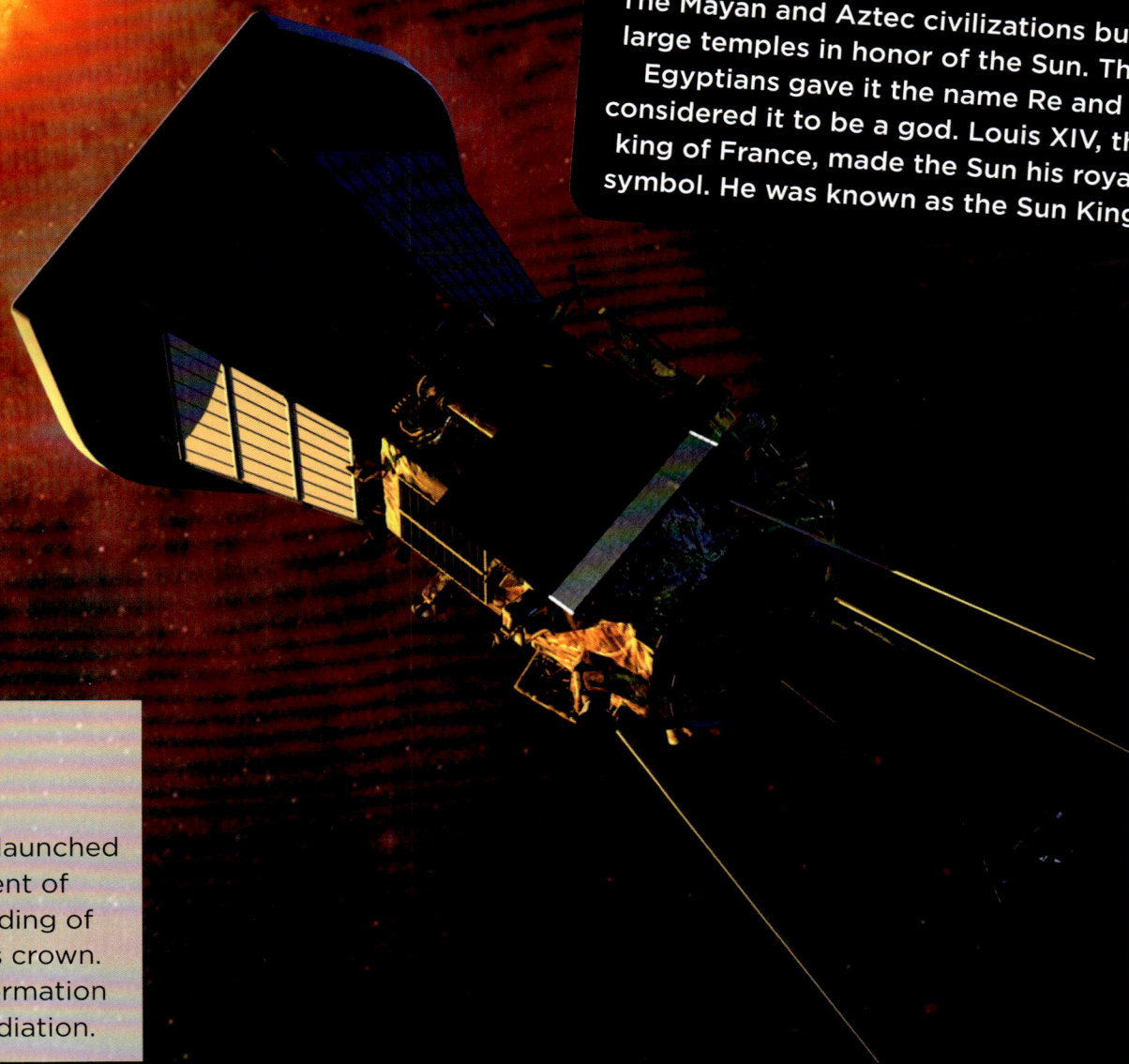

SDO/AIA 171   2015-09-13 07:12:23 UT

SOLAR ECLIPSES

A solar eclipse occurs when the Moon comes between the Sun and the Earth. A total eclipse occurs very rarely and cannot be observed at all locations on Earth at the same time.

Beware! It is dangerous to look at a solar eclipse with the naked eye. You need special equipment to be able to observe one under safe conditions.

SOLAR PANELS

The cells contained in these panels convert the rays of the Sun into electricity. These solar panels are recognized by their dark blue color.

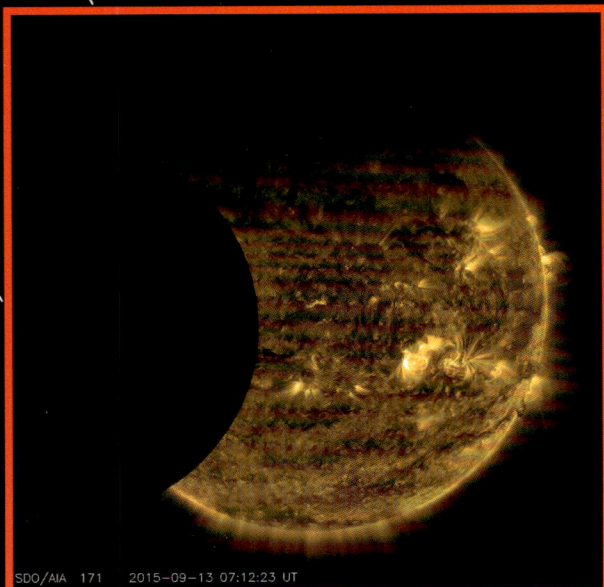

21

MERCURY

The smallest planet of our solar system is the closest one to the Sun and also the hottest! The rocky surface of Mercury is characterized by craters, formed by the impact of thousands of meteorites. The enormous iron core of the planet represents more than 75% of its mass.

Diameter: 4,878 km (3,031 mi.)

Orbital period: 88 Earth days

Average distance from the Sun: 58 million km (36 million mi.)

Surface temperature: between 430 °C and -180 °C (806 °F and -292 °F)

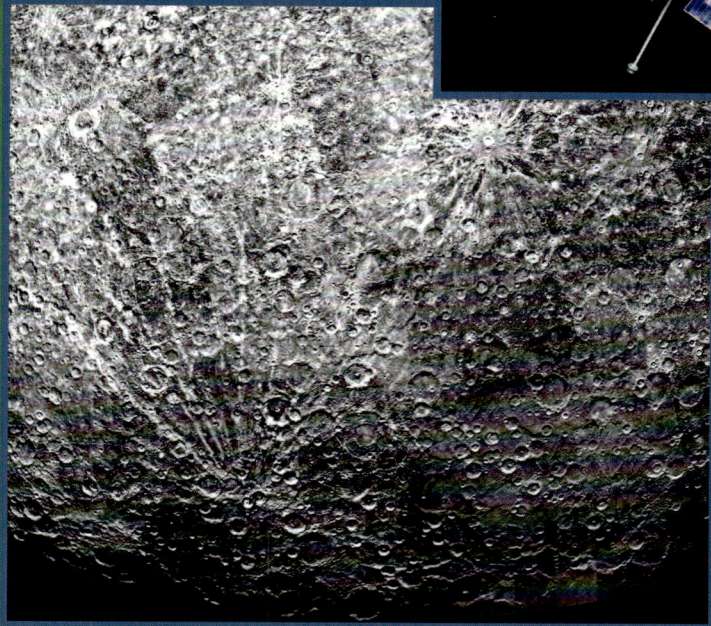

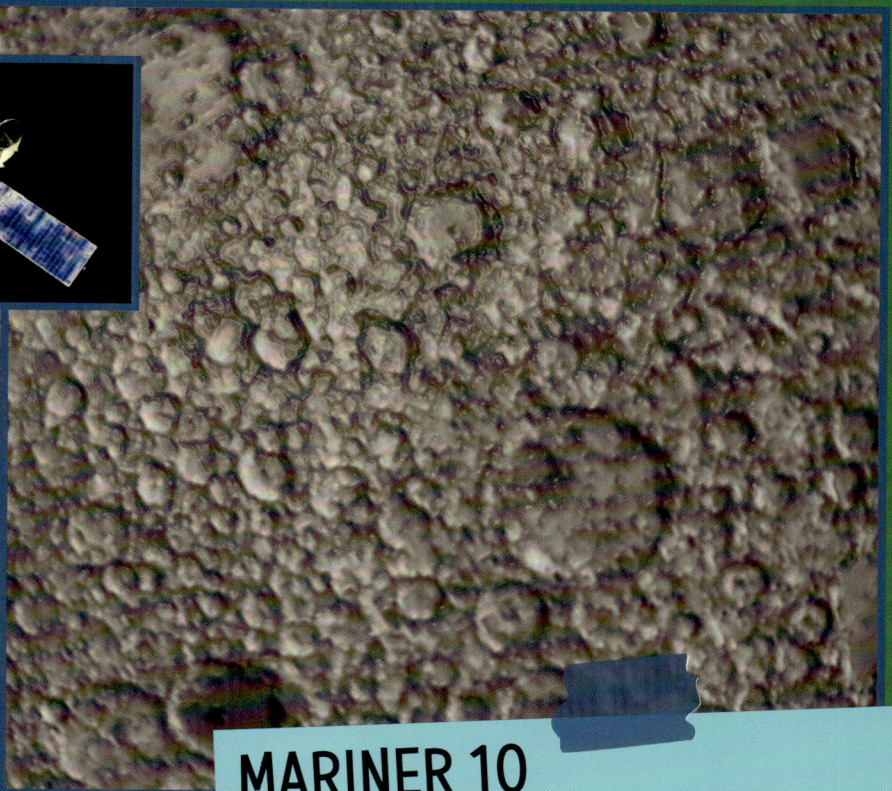

MARINER 10

In 1974 and 1975, the probe was launched by NASA, and completed three flights around Mercury. For the first time, astronomers were able to see its surface in detail, which looked a lot like the surface of the Moon. *Mariner 10* is the first probe to be used by the assistance of the gravitational field. The navigation system used the **planet's gravitational force** to modify its trajectory.

EXPLORING MERCURY

Up until recently, Mercury was one of the least explored planets in our solar system. It is also difficult to observe it from Earth. To this day, two probes have been sent with a mission to study this planet.

MESSENGER

More than 30 years after the first mission towards Mercury, NASA launched, the *MESSENGER* probe in 2004. The goal was to send the probe into orbit around the planet and to capture a complete picture of it. In 2015, after 4 years of being in orbit, *MESSENGER* crashed on the surface of Mercury, however it had already captured a large quantity of information.

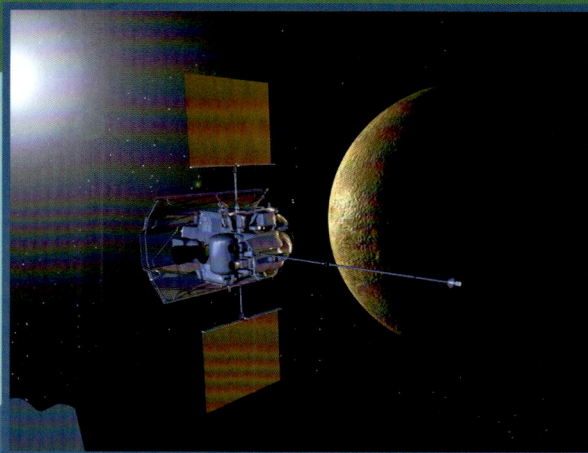

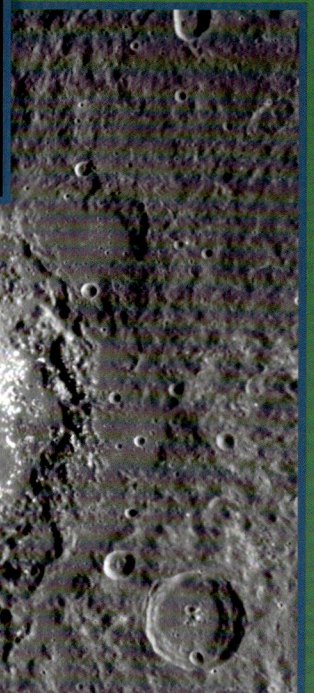

OBSERVING MERCURY

With binoculars or a telescope, we can locate the planet **near the horizon** at dawn or dusk. Like the Moon, Mercury has its own phases. It is most visible at its furthest point from the Sun.

VENUS

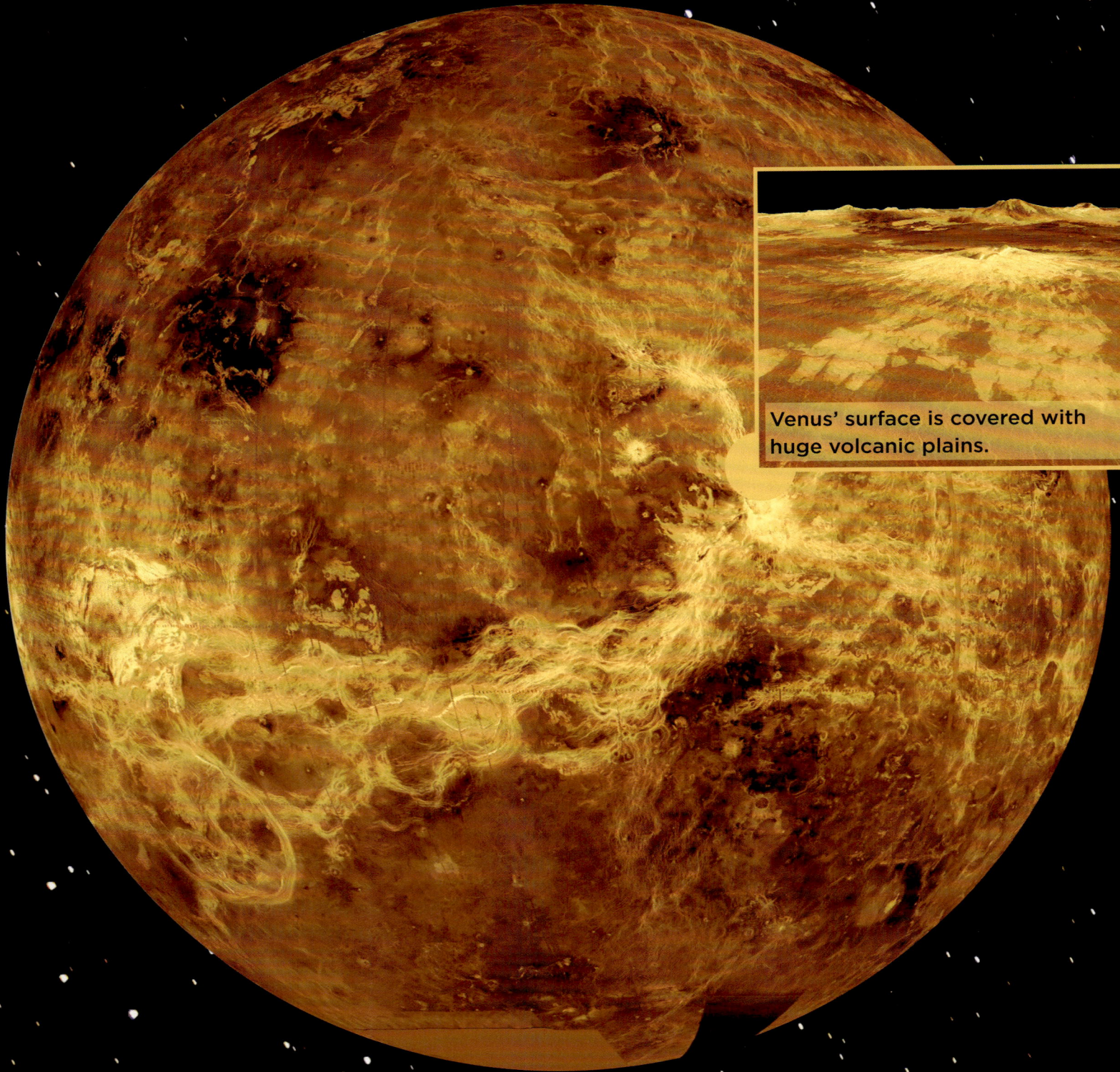

Venus' surface is covered with huge volcanic plains.

Venus is an arid planet, meaning it lacks water. Its temperatures are infernal! Its atmosphere made up of dense clouds traps the sun's ultraviolet rays. The carbon dioxide that it's composed of causes a greenhouse gas effect.

Diameter: 12,102 km (7,519 mi.)

Orbital period: 224.7 Earth days

Average distance from the Sun: 108 million km (67 million mi.)

Surface temperature: 464 °C (867 °F)

EXPLORING VENUS

Did you know?

Venera 7 is the first machine to have landed successfully on another planet. For 23 minutes, the Soviet probe recorded and sent precious information back to Earth until the immense atmospheric pressure and extreme temperatures of Venus destroyed it.

MARINER 2

In 1962, the American probe *Mariner 2* flew over Venus. During this flight, information from another planet was sent back to Earth for the first time ever.

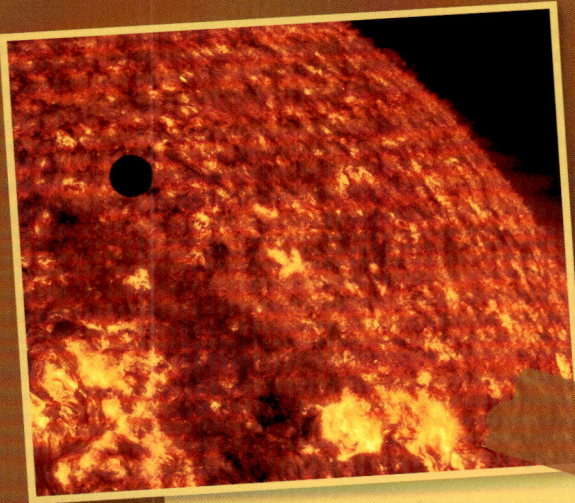

OBSERVING VENUS

Venus is the **brightest object in our sky**, after the Sun and the Moon. This is due to two factors: its proximity to Earth and its atmosphere. The clouds of Venus reflect the rays of the Sun. Its nickname is the shepherd's star, even though it is not a star. We see it shine in the sky after sunset.

MAGELLAN

In 1989, the space shuttle *Atlantis* launched the *Magellan* probe to Venus. This NASA probe's mission was to **map** the surface. This allowed astronomers to discover volcanoes, expansive plains and some special areas that make up Venus's landscape.

25

MARS

For ages, the planet Mars has inspired writers and fascinated astronomers. Martians, as we have imaged them in movies, have never existed. However, this has never stopped scientists from continuing their search for traces of microscopic life on the red planet.

Diameter: 6,796 km (4,222 mi.)

Orbital period: 687 Earth days

Average distance from the Sun: 228 million km (141,6 million mi.)

Surface temperature: -62 °C (79 °F)

EXPLORING MARS

We think that Mars was once hot and humid and that water may have run in great abundance. Up to today, we have discovered water in solid form (ice) and gas (vapor) in parts of the planet that are little exposed to the Sun.

CURIOSITY

The **Curiosity rover** has been traveling the surface on the Gale crater since 2012. This laboratory on wheels is the size of a car and is equipped with 2-meter (6.5 ft.) long arms. Its mission is to determine if there was ever life on Mars.

VIKING 1 AND 2

American probes were the first to successfully **land** on the planet. They send back images and analysis information on the composition of the surface and the atmosphere.

MARS PATHFINDER

In 1997, the United-States landed the first **motorized vehicle** on the surface of Mars. Its giant parachute and airbag system safely landed the vehicle. This vehicle was controlled at a distance by NASA scientists. It transported instruments that allow analyses to be performed.

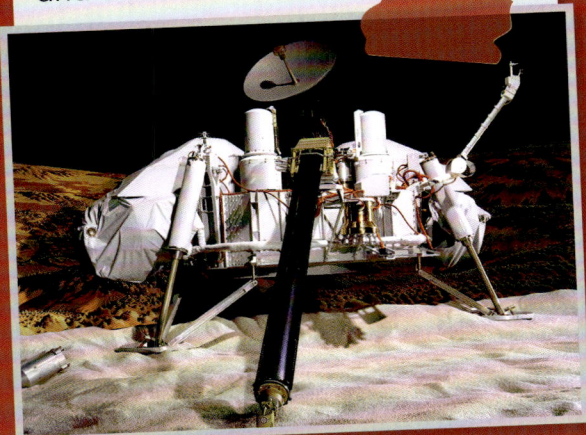

27

JUPITER

JUNO

53 (16 to be confirmed) natural satellites.

Jupiter's largest moon, Ganymede, measures 5,268 km (3,273 mi.) in diameter. It is therefore larger than the planet Mercury.

Imagine a planet so large that it could contain 1,300 Earths. Jupiter is the largest planet in our solar system. This gas giant does not have a solid surface. It is formed of layers of clouds and liquid gas. It also has a small iron core.

Diameter: 142,984 km (88,846 mi.)

Orbital period: 4,330 Earth days

Average distance from the Sun: 778.4 million km (483.6 million mi.)

Surface temperature: -148 °C (-91.9 °F)

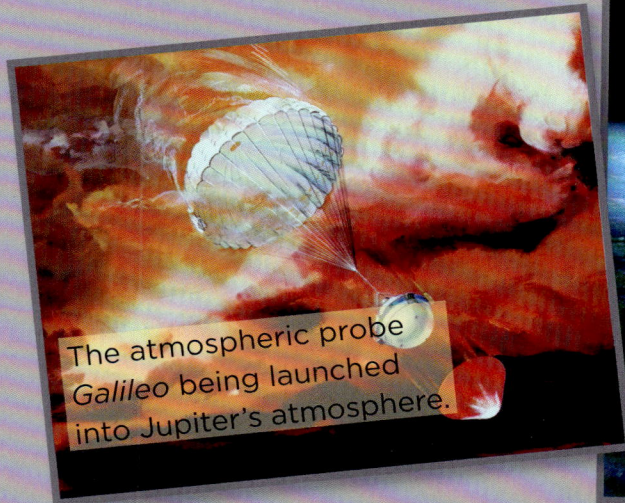

The atmospheric probe *Galileo* being launched into Jupiter's atmosphere.

GALILEO

Launched in 1989, this spacecraft entered into Jupiter's orbit in 1995. During its 34 orbits around Jupiter, for the first time, the probe would study the composition of this planet's atmosphere. It discovered **traces of water** on its moons, Europa, Ganymede and Callisto. The American probe's mission lasted 14 years.

JUNO

Launched in 2011, the *Juno* probe took five years to reach its destination. Its mission was to study the composition of Jupiter's **atmosphere**. *Juno* allowed us to better understand the structure of this planet and how it was formed.

GALILEO'S SATELLITES

Over fifty natural satellites gravitate around Jupiter. The four largest were discovered in 1610 by Galileo. These moons are called Io, Europa, Ganymede and Callisto.

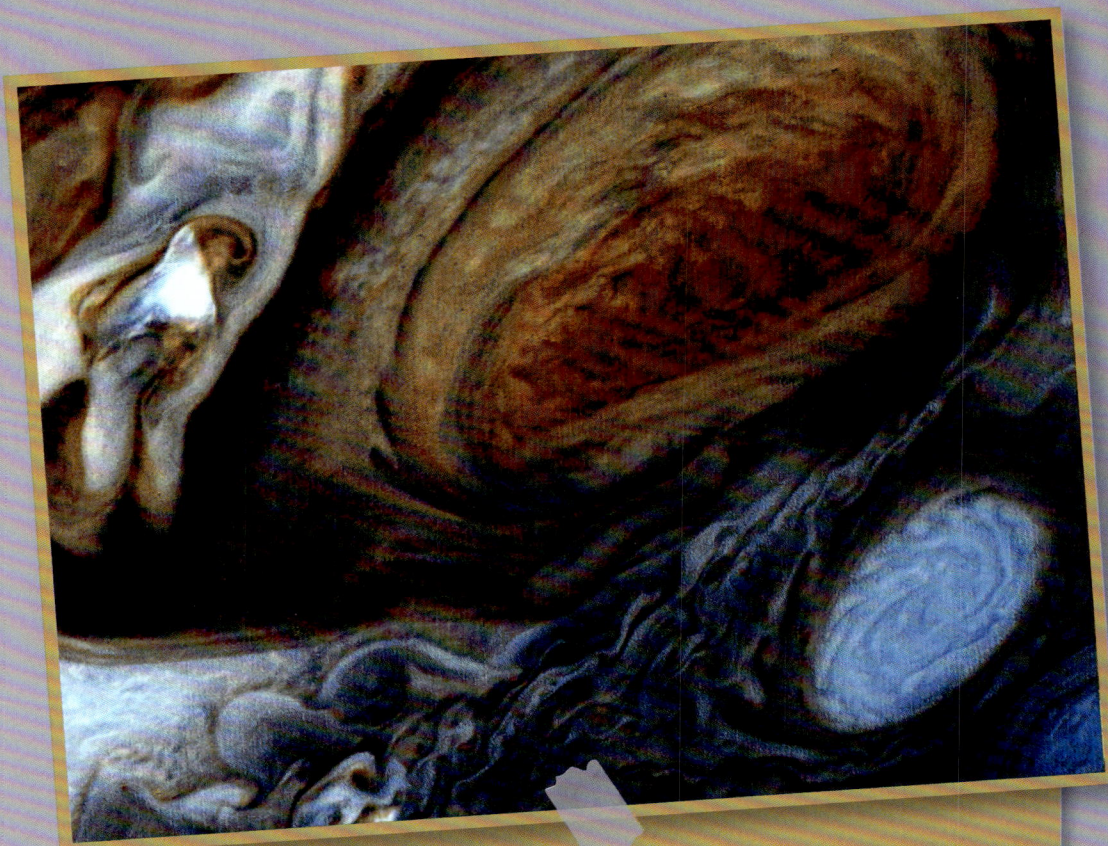

THE RED SPOT

Three hundred fifty years ago, Robert Hooke discovered a very large red spot on the surface of Jupiter. This phenomenon is actually caused by a **super hurricane**. This hurricane is so large, it measures twice the size of Earth. The storms that form on Jupiter can last several hundreds of years.

SATURN

53 (9 to be confirmed) natural satellites.

Like the other gas giants, Saturn does not have a solid surface. It is mainly composed of clouds of gas and water. The winds that blow on Saturn can reach a speed of more than 1,800 km/h (1,118 mph.) By comparison, the strongest winds ever registered on Earth have reached only 408 km/h (253 mph.).

Diameter: 120,536 km (74,897 mi.)

Orbital period: 10,756 Earth days

Average distance from the Sun: 1.43 billion km (888.5 million mi.)

Surface temperature: -177 °C (-286.6 °F)

EXPLORING SATURN

The probe *Pioneer 11* is the first to explore Saturn during its flight around the planet in 1979.

THE RINGS OF SATURN

The rings of Saturn are composed of billions of **rock and ice particles**. These reflect the light and become so bright that they are easily observable. The size of these particles can vary greatly. Some are the size of dust. Others are the **size of mountains**. Scientists have not yet found out how these rings were formed. These may be the remains of comets or the result of a collision between Saturn and a natural satellite.

Did you know?

Astronomers named the rings of Saturn by the letters A to G. In 1675, Jean Dominique Cassini was the first to note the separation between rings A and B. The other rings were discovered in the following centuries.

CASSINI-HUYGENS

To be placed in orbit around Saturn, the *Cassini* probe had to pass **between two rings**. *Cassini* was the first terrestrial spacecraft selected to study Saturn. It completed 74 orbits around the planet. Its mission ended 20 years after its launch. Thanks to *Cassini*, the scientific community unlocked several of Saturn's secrets and mysteries.

In 2005, a probe from the European Space Agency, carried by *Cassini*, landed on the largest of Saturn's moons, **Titan**. *Cassini-Huygens's* probes took **6.7 years** to travel towards Saturn. The probe's descent toward Titan was achieved with a parachute and lasted more than 2 hours. Once it had landed on the surface of Titan, *Huygens* performed measurements on the ground for 1 hour before shutting down.

URANUS

27 natural satellites.

It is only in 1781 that a German astronomer, William Herschel, discovered the existence of Uranus. For a long time, it was believed to be a star since its movement in the sky was observed to be very slow. It takes 84 years to circle around the Sun!

Uranus is a very cold and mysterious planet. The planet measures four times the diameter of Earth. It is however more than twenty times further from the Sun than our planet. At this distance from the Sun, the light that reaches Uranus is not sufficient to warm it. Its surface temperature is the same on the side that is exposed to the Sun as it is to the side that is hidden from it.

Diameter: 51,118 km (31,763 mi.)

Orbital period: 30,687 Earth days

Average distance from the Sun: 2.87 billion km (1.78 billion mi.)

Surface temperature: -224 °C (-371 °F)

EXPLORING URANUS

We knew very little about Uranus as a planet before the flight of the probe *Voyager 2*. To this day, it is the only spacecraft that has approached the ice giant.

VOYAGER 2

Launched in 1977, *Voyager 2*'s mission was to explore the four furthest planets of the solar system. It was a very ambitious project for NASA. It wasn't until 1986 that the probe *Voyager 2* flew over the planet Uranus. In 9 years, *Voyager 2* traveled billions of kilometers in space to reach the ice giant. From this distance, the probe communicated by **radio signals** that took 2.5 hours to reach Earth.

Voyager 2 allowed scientists to discover 10 new moons and new rings. The probe also sent back several extraordinary photos of this distant world.

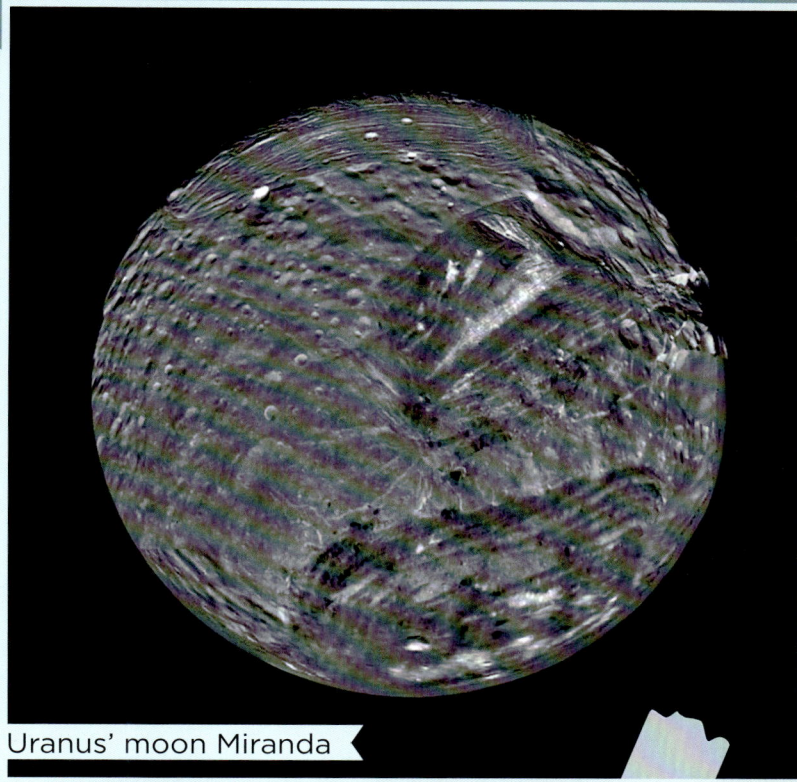

Uranus' moon Miranda

AN ICE GIANT

Uranus has no solid surface, just like the other gas planets. However, under a layer of clouds, **gases slowly transform into liquid**. Its rocky or solid ice center make it denser than its giant cousins. We call Uranus and Neptune "ice giants".

NEPTUNE

13 natural satellites.

The planet that is the furthest from the Sun takes its name from the roman god of the seas. The dark blue color of the planet reminds one of the deep oceans. Neptune looks a lot like Uranus, more than it does the other gaseous planets. They are almost identical in size and very similar in composition. It is made up of gases with a rocky and icy center.

34

Diameter: 49,528 km (30,775 mi.)

Orbital period: 59,790 Earth days

Average distance from the Sun: 4.49 billion km (2.78 billion mi.)

Surface temperature: -214 °C (-353 °F)

EXPLORING NEPTUNE

THE DISCOVERY OF NEPTUNE

Neptune was the first planet to be discovered through **calculations** and not by observation. In the 1800's, a French mathematician, Alexis Bouvard, observed Uranus' orbit. He noticed a slight deviation from its trajectory.

One of the explanations for this phenomenon was the presence of another planet. About 50 years later, it was proved that his hypothesis was correct. There was indeed an eighth planet in our solar system.

Triton

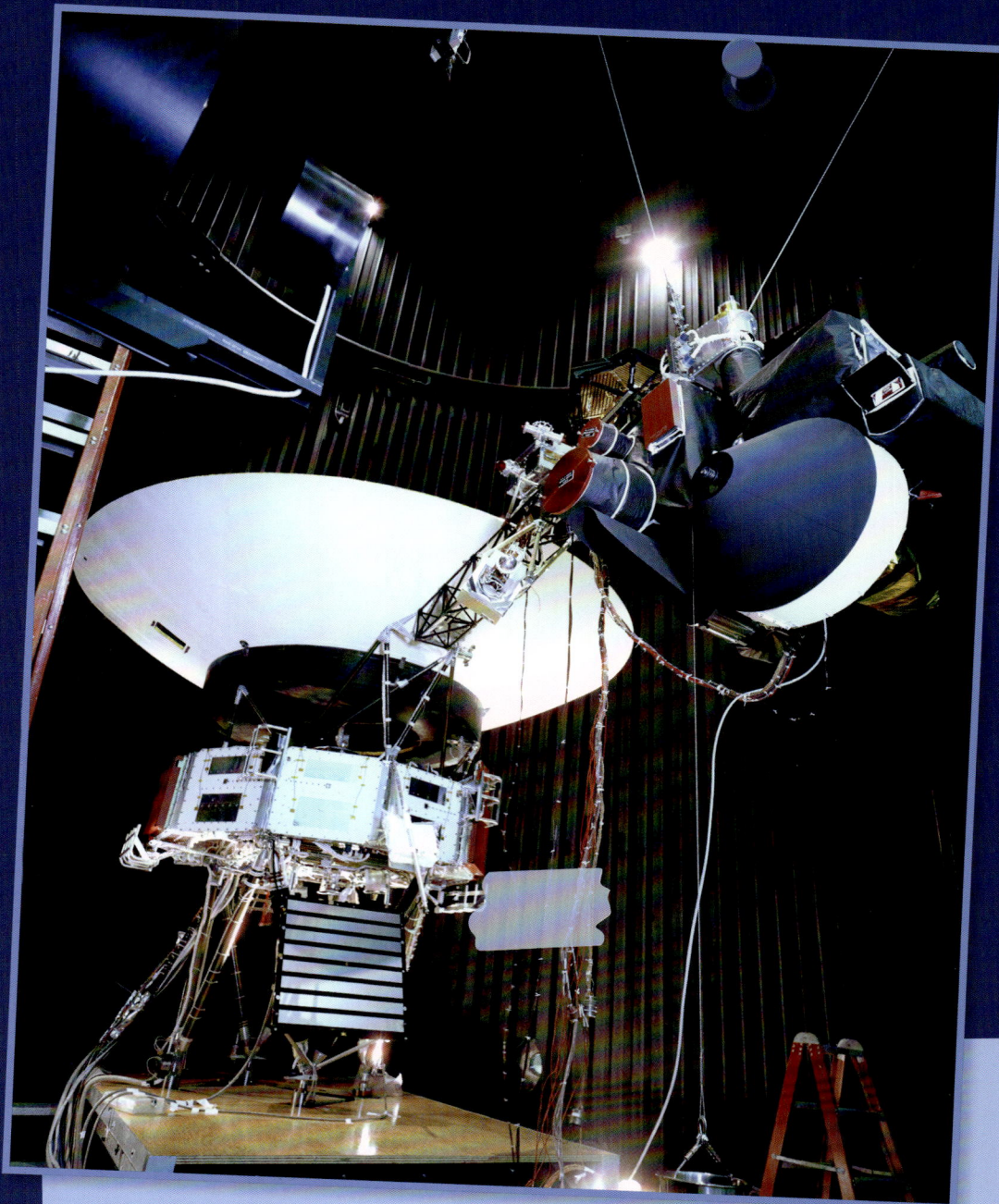

VOYAGER 2

As in the case of Uranus, the only probe that visited Neptune was *Voyager 2*. After traveling more than **7 billion kilometers** (4.34 billion miles), this probe was able to fly over the ice giant. It discovered more than five new moons as well as four rings. Similar to all the giant planets, Neptune has a series of rings that gravitate around it. However, these cannot be seen from Earth.

At the moment, there are no other space missions planned to fly over Neptune. *Voyager 2* continues its travel in space, more than 40 years after its start from Earth.

THE STARS

There are billions of stars similar to the Sun in the universe. These giant stars gravitate several thousands of light years from our planet. The energy that emanates is such that we can perceive them from their light. The energy travels unimaginable distances through space to reach us.

THE BIRTH OF A STAR

The Orion nebula

Stars are born in giant clouds of gas and dust. We call these clouds nebulae. In many ways, these are star nurseries.

The Orion nebula holds several young stars. It was discovered in 1610 by Nicolas-Claude Fabri de Peiresc. It is the nebula that is the most easily observable from Earth.

A blue proto-star

The nebula is divided into smaller clouds. These contract under the effect of gravitation. The star that forms is called a "proto-star".

Proto-stars in nebulae

At this stage, the proto-star begins to spin very quickly on itself. It sucks gases and dust that form a larger and larger disk around it.

Within the new star, two opposing phenomena occur. At the center of the young star, things are very unstable. The gravitational force forces it to contract. The energy that is released tries to make its way externally. This stage of the formation is called "T Tauri".

The creation of a new star

After millions of years, the internal forces of the star reach equilibrium. This means that it has reached its "main sequence". At this point, its stage is very much like that of an adult in life. This is the longest and most stable stage in its existence. Our Sun is currently in this part of its development.

The red dwarf

This is an illustration of the spectacular red dwarf explosion. Red dwarfs are among the most common stars in space.

THE DEATH OF A STAR

After thousands of years, the star begins to transform itself again. These changes are determined by its mass and size.

A brown dwarf

SMALL MASS

A star with small mass shrinks slowly and ends up extinguishing completely. It becomes what we call a "brown dwarf". Brown dwarfs are very difficult to identify. We are able to detect them with the help of the infrared rays that they emit.

AVERAGE MASS

The Helix nebula

A star with an average mass (such as the Sun) swells and becomes red. We call it a "red giant". It can stay in this stage for billions of years. Once all the reserves of gas have been spent, the red giant ejects a large quantity of matter into space. The ejected matter becomes a "planetary nebula". The Helix nebula is one of the closest to Earth.

Sirius B

After the star loses its external layers, nothing remains except its core. The core of the former star is called the white dwarf. The white dwarf loses its shine very slowly and begins to become difficult to be observed from Earth. We estimate that 96% of stars in our galaxy will become white dwarfs.

38

LARGE MASS

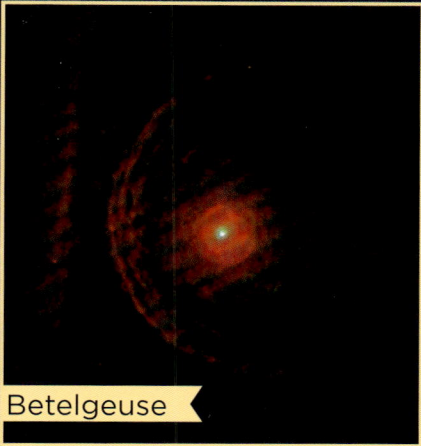
Betelgeuse

A star with a large mass will enlarge and become a very large star that we call a supergiant. Supergiant stars are very bright. Betelgeuse is a supergiant red star that is 1000 times larger than the Sun.

The Crab nebula

At the end of its life, a supergiant star suddenly ejects matter into space. It's a very intense phenomenon that releases a large quantity of energy. The spectacular explosions are called "supernovae". These occur very rarely and are only infrequently observed.

The Crab nebula, located in the Taurus constellation, is the remnants of a supernova.

Neutron star

After the explosion of a supergiant, nothing remains except for its dense and compact core. This is what we call a "neutron star". Neutron stars measure a few dozen kilometers (miles) in diameter.

Did you know?

At the center of galaxies are supermassive black holes. A giant black hole, that is located at the center of our galaxy, is a few million times more massive than the Sun.

CONSTELLATIONS

For ages, humans have observed the night sky with great interest. They have devised many new formations by observing the stars. A constellation is a group of stars gathered together by imaginary lines. These constellations form particular figures that we attribute a meaning to.

Ptolemy

Each civilization interpreted the skies in their own way. For example, in ancient China, constellations were divided into 7 houses. In India, they divided the sky into 27 sections, closely tied to the Hindu calendar. In the 1920s, the International Astronomical Union (IAU) standardized the observation of the skies. They divided the sky into 88 constellations. The IAU defined the form and the borders of each of these.

Ptolemy, a Greek astronomer, who lived almost 2,000 years ago, wrote many papers on astronomy. In one of his works, he details 48 constellations. These would later be adopted by the IAU as they were conceptualized by Ptolemy. They are known as the "constellations of Ptolemy".

In astrology, each sign of the zodiac corresponds to a constellation. The twelve constellations of the zodiac are Aries, Taurus, Gemini, Cancer, Leo, Virgo, Libra, Scorpio, Sagittarius, Capricorn, Aquarius, and Pisces. These constellations also make up the constellations of Ptolemy.

SEEN FROM EARTH

The image that we have of the sky depends on where we are located. Where we are gives us a different perspective of the sky. The visible constellations in the Northern hemisphere are different from the ones in the Southern hemisphere.

Since the Earth moves around the Sun, the night sky changes with the seasons. Some constellations are visible only during a certain period of the year.

If we observe the sky from the North and the South poles, certain constellations may be visible all year long. We call these the "circumpolar constellations". In the Northern hemisphere, it is the constellations that are closest to the North star. In the Southern hemisphere, we find these near the constellation called the Southern Cross.

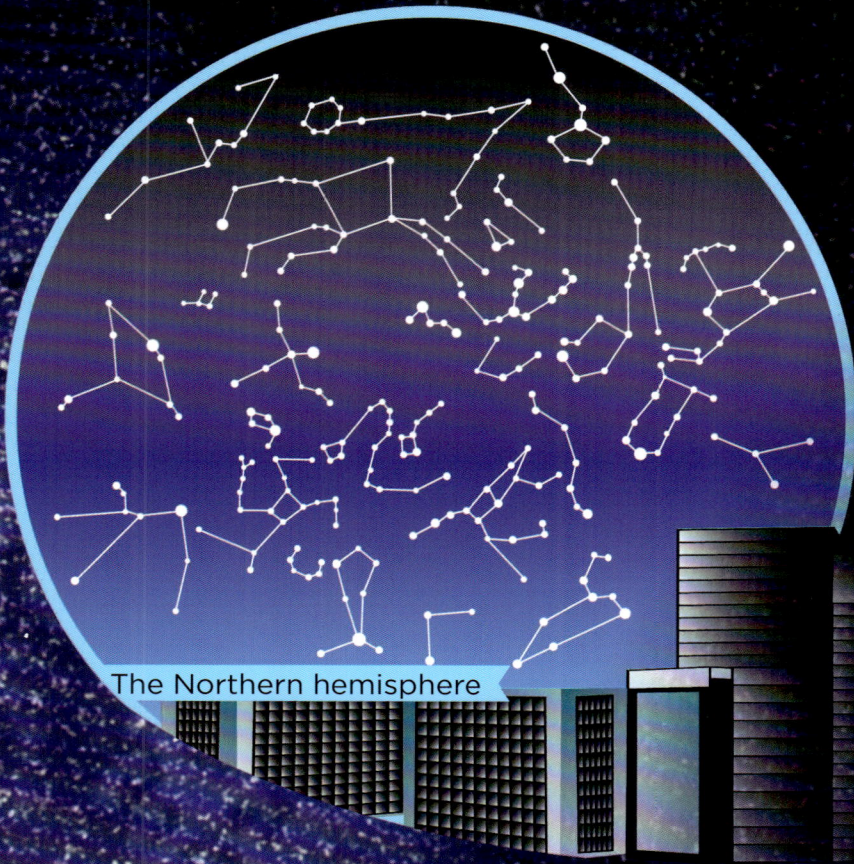

The Northern hemisphere

OBSERVING THE SKY

Several constellations are visible with the naked eye, with binoculars or with an amateur telescope. It is always preferable to observe stars from the countryside, far away from light pollution emanating from the cities. Furthermore, visibility is always better in winter since the air is dryer. The evenings during which there is a new moon are best for observing the night sky.

THE GREAT BEAR

Its seven bright stars allow us to easily recognize its saucepan-like shape. This constellation is the most well-known and one of the more easily identifiable. Dubhe, the brightest star in this constellation, is an orange supergiant. We estimate that it is about 30 times bigger than our Sun.

THE SMALL BEAR

This constellation looks like a small saucepan. The North star can be seen at the end of the curved arm.

THE DRAGON

This constellation is made up of a long line of stars. None of them are very bright, which makes the Dragon more difficult to see. Notice the two eyes, one of which is the giant orange star called Etamin. The other is a supergiant called Rastaban.

ANDROMEDA

The shape of Andromeda reminds us of the letter A. Its brightest star is called Alpheratz. It is 110 times brighter than our Sun.

CEPHEUS

The shape of Cepheus resembles a pentagon or a house drawn by a child. The brightest star of the constellation is called Alderamin.

CASSIOPEIA

This constellation is in the shape of the letter W. We can find the North Star from Cassiopeia, at the continuation of the central point of the shape of the W.

THE LYRA

The most visible star in this constellation is Vega. It is the fifth brightest star in the sky. Vega was the first star to be photographed in 1850.

PERSEUS

Known since the Antiquities, this constellation is named after the mythological hero that saved Andromeda. It contains several bright stars such as Algol.

THE LIZARD

Located between Cassiopeia and the Swan, the Lizard can be recognized by its zigzag shape. We can see it when the sky is clear.

THE SWAN

This constellation, also called the "Northern Cross," has the shape of a cross. Since many of its stars are very bright, we use it to locate other constellations around it. Its brightest star, Deneb, is located at its head.

TRIANGLE

4 ANDROMEDA

9 LIZARD

10 SWAN

6 CASSIOPEIA

8 PERSEUS

5 CEPHEUS

GIRAFFE

7 LYRA

2 THE SMALL BEAR

LYNX

HERCULES

3 DRAGON

BOUVIER

1 THE GREAT BEAR

THE GALAXIES

Galaxies are made of gas, dark matter, dust and stars. Massive black holes are found at their center. These enormous structures are tied together by the force of gravity. Scientists believe there are more than 10 trillion galaxies in the universe!

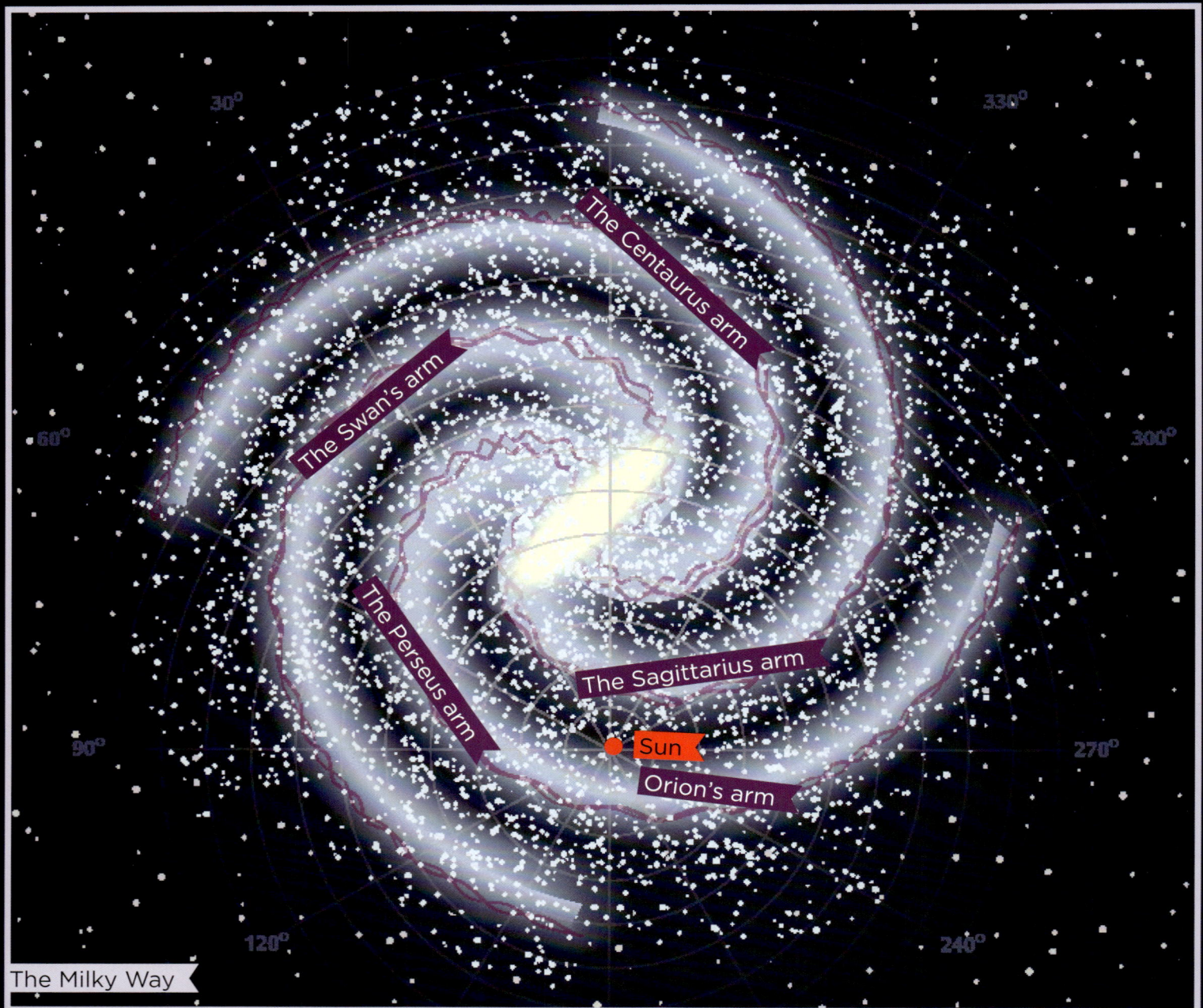

The Milky Way

THE MILKY WAY

Observing the night's sky, far away from the cities, we can see a long, white trail passing through the horizon. This bright dust is actually part of an arm of our galaxy.

44

The Milky Way is our galaxy. It contains more than 100 billion stars. Just like our sun, many of these stars have their own planetary system. The Milky Way stretches well beyond the human imagination. Its diameter is estimated to be 100,000 light years.

The Milky Way is a galaxy in the shape of a barred spiral. Our solar system is located in Orion's arm.

DIFFERENT TYPES OF GALAXIES

Astronomers divide the galaxies into five categories:

Did you know?

Our planet turns on its axis and around the Sun. Our solar system also rotates within our galaxy.

Elliptical

Spiral

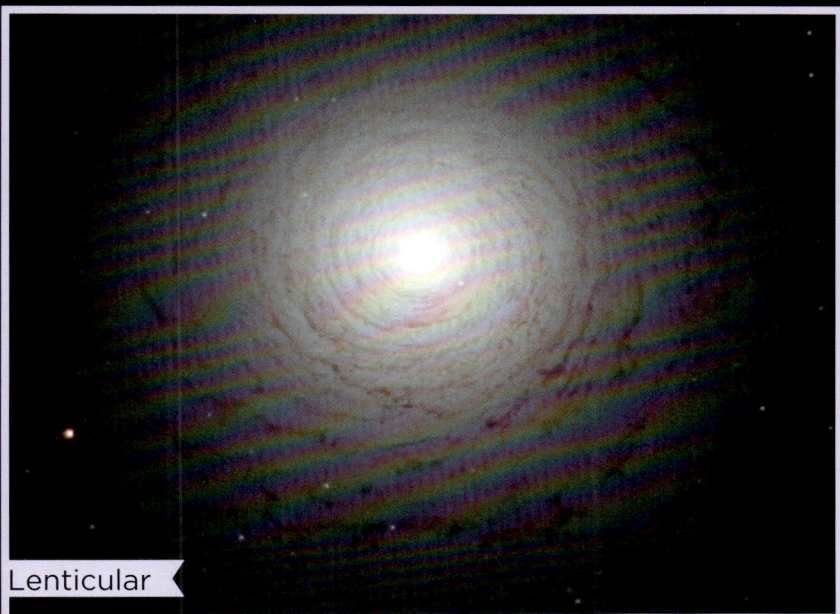

Lenticular

Barred spiral

Irregular

THE LEGEND OF THE MILKY WAY

In Greek mythology, Zeus, the king of gods, had a child. He wanted to make his child immortal by having it drink from his wife's breast, the goddess Hera. He placed the child next to her breast while she slept. When she awoke, she was surprised and pushed the baby in such a way that the milk spilled. This is how we explain the white traces that make up the Milky Way in the night sky.

45

THE HISTORY OF THE ROCKET

The rocket was a Chinese invention that dates more than 800 years. The first rockets looked like arrows powered by the explosions of powder.

1 The Chinese used gunpowder against the Mongols during war time. The Mongols picked up this idea and perfected it. It is due to the Mongol empire that the rocket spread across all of Europe.

2 In the 16th century, a German pyrotechnic called Johann Schmidlap, devised a system that could allow fireworks to reach higher altitudes. These rockets were made in two parts. The bottom rocket, the biggest part, propels the top rocket, which is smaller. When the bottom rocket has finished burning, the smaller rocket continues its ascension. The principle behind this is still used in the construction of modern rockets today.

3 Writers such as Carl Sagan and Jules Verne have also participated, in their own way, to the development of space technologies. In their stories, characters visited the Moon and the planet Mars. They traveled on spacecrafts pulled by giant swans or propelled by canons.

4 In 1902, Georges Melies produced a science-fiction movie called *A Trip to the Moon.*

Modern rocket

Konstantin Tsiolkovsky

5 At the end of the 19th century, the Russian Konstantin Tsiolkovsky formulated new theories. He proposed the use of liquid fuels to replace canon powder. Even though he never built a rocket in his lifetime, his theories are at the heart of the invention of modern rockets.

6 The American Robert Goddard dedicated his life to the invention of rockets. On March 16, 1926, he performed his first trial of a rocket using liquid fuels. His rocket, Goddard 1, reached a height of 12.5 meters (41 ft.). This first launch was a success. Between 1926 to 1941, he completed several trials with his increasingly powerful engines.

7 The Second World War accelerated the advancement of new technologies. German scientists developed a powerful missile. The V2 was able to fly higher than any other rocket built before it. At the end of the War, several German engineers were recruited by the United States. This launched the beginning of the American space program.

8 Wernher von Braun, the inventor of the V2 rocket under the German Nazis, emigrated to the United States. Thanks to his rocket, the Saturn 5, man was able to walk on the Moon.

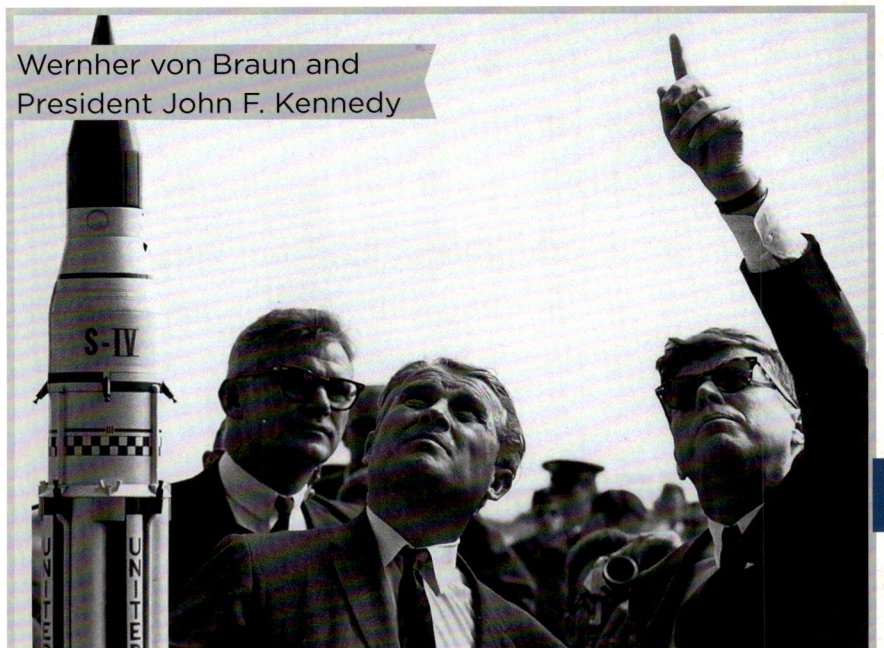

Wernher von Braun and President John F. Kennedy

THE SPACE RACE

In the 1950s, the United States and the Soviet Union began a relentless race. For these two superpowers, space was the new frontier to conquer and any scientific advancements would become state secrets. These two nations began a race to conquer space.

October 4, 1957

SPUTNIK 1
The first artificial satellite is put into orbit around Earth by the Soviets.

November 3, 1957

SPUTNIK 2
The dog Laika became the first living being to orbit Earth on board a Soviet satellite.

December 14, 1961

VOSTOK
Yuri Gagarine became the first man to go into space. He completed a full orbit around Earth before returning back safely.

December 14, 1962

MARINER 2
The American probe flies over Venus. It's the first visit of another planet by a terrestrial engine.

| 1957 | 1958 | 1959 | 1960 | 1961 | 1962 |

December 18, 1958

SCORE
The first satellite built for telecommunications was deployed by the Americans.

January 4, 1959

LUNA 1
The Soviet probe completes its flight over the Moon. A few months later, Luna 2 lands on the Moon.

TIROS
The first meteorological satellite took its first televised photo of Earth.

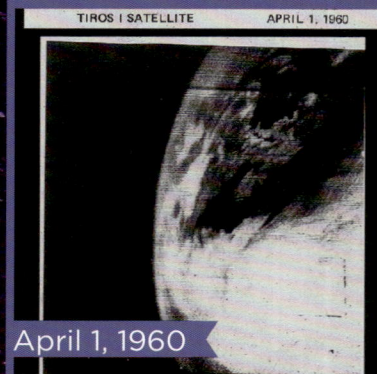

April 1, 1960

July 21, 1969

APOLLO 11
Neil Armstrong and Buzz Aldrin walk on the Moon.

THE APOLLO-SOYUZ MISSION

The United-States and the Soviet Union prepared a shared mission and joined their resources as well as their knowledge for the first time. In 1975, American and Soviet spacecrafts joined together in space. It was the beginning of a new cooperation.

The Russian Valeri Polyakov spent 14 months on the Mir space station. It is recorded as the longest space mission to date.

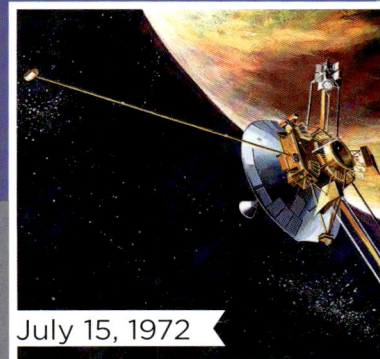

July 15, 1972

PIONEER 10
The American probe penetrates the main asteroid belt.

| 1965 | 1968 | 1969 | 1970 | 1971 | 1972 |

March 18, 1965

VOSKHOD
Alexei Leonov completes a spacewalk from a space shuttle.

December 21, 1968

APOLLO 8
The members aboard the American spaceship were the first humans to see the hidden side of the Moon.

November 23, 1970

LUNOKHOD 1
The Russian motorized probe is the first of its kind to cross the surface of the Moon.

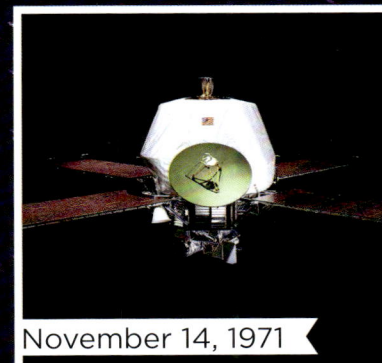

November 14, 1971

MARINER 9
The Americans launch a probe around Mars's orbit.

THE INTERNATIONAL
SPACE STATION

The International Space Station (ISS) is a laboratory in orbit around Earth. The ISS is a collaborative project between the space agencies of the United-States, Canada, Japan, Russia and Europe. It is the brightest object in our night sky, after the Moon. It is the largest bright point that moves at regular speed.

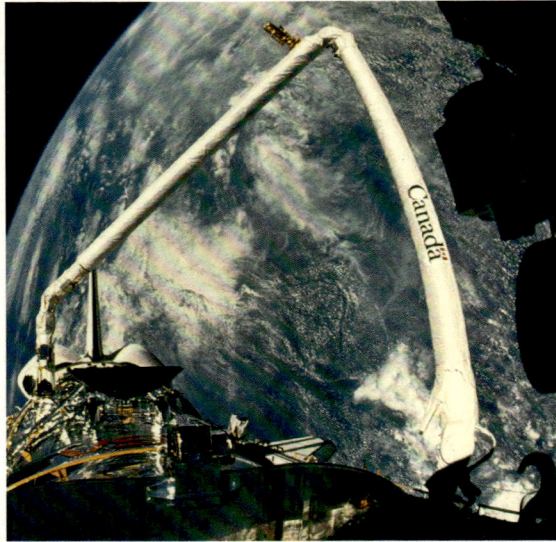

The ISS welcomes scientists from several countries. They perform experiments under conditions that do not exist on Earth. The discoveries made on the ISS help to improve quality of life on Earth.

The International Space Station travels around Earth in 90 minutes. It moves at a speed of 28,000 km/h (17,400 mph)!

This enormous structure is in orbit at an altitude of 370 km (230 mi.) from Earth. The ISS measures about one football field in length, that is 109 m by 61 m (357 ft. by 200 ft.).

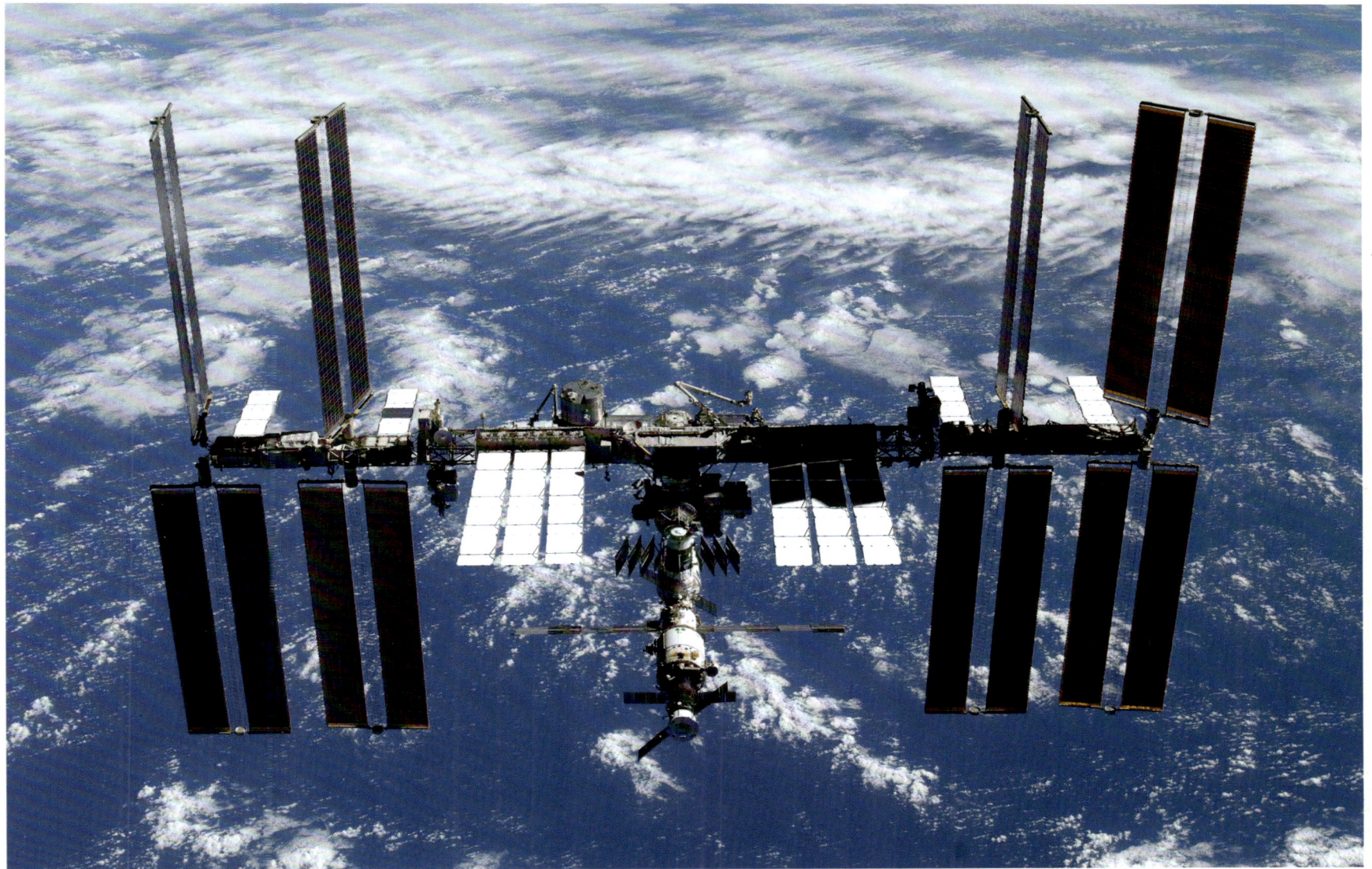

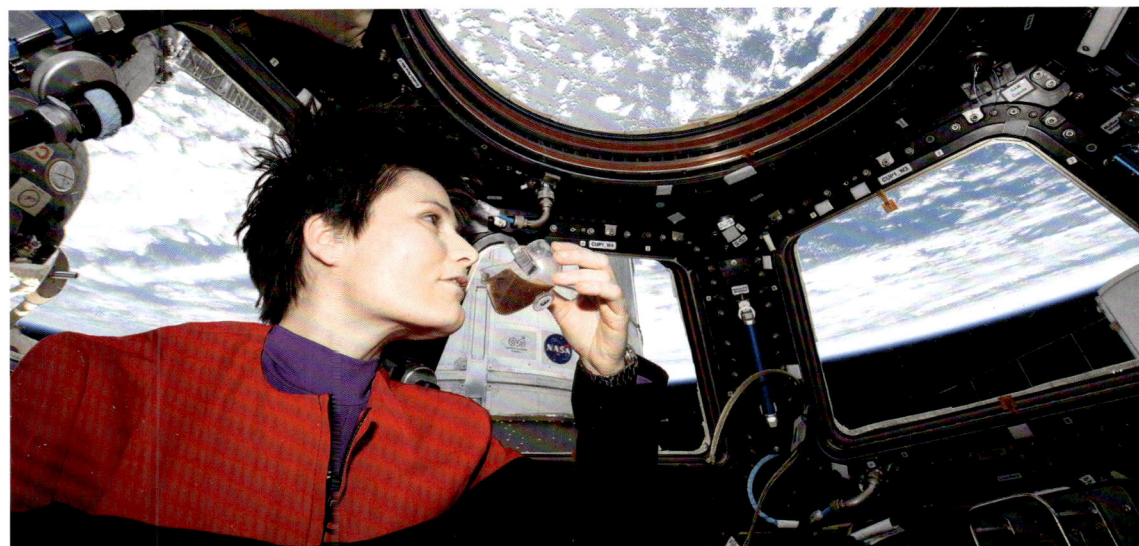

The ISS can hold up to 6 crew members and is supplied by cargo vessels. Missions aboard the ISS generally last 2 weeks to 6 months.

THE ASTRONAUTS

Aspiring astronauts have to be in excellent physical condition. They must have specific qualities to be able to live and work under extreme conditions. Often times, these are pilots, doctors, engineers or scientists. They are selected among thousands of candidates.

1 DEVELOPMENT

Astronauts follow an **intensive development program** before their trip into space. Preparation includes several phases and generally lasts two years.

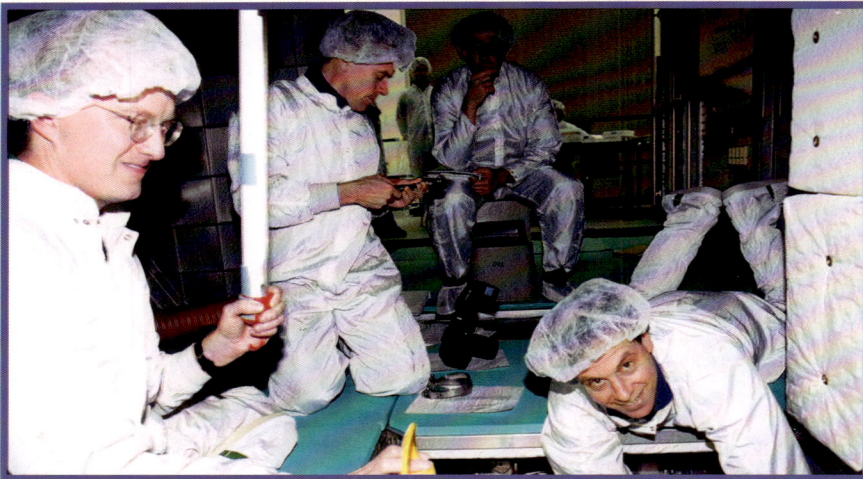

2 TECHNICAL TRAINING

Aspiring astronauts follow technical training of all kinds before their mission into space. They also prepare to perform **scientific experiments** in orbit. They must also know how to operate and pilot the machinery and spacecraft.

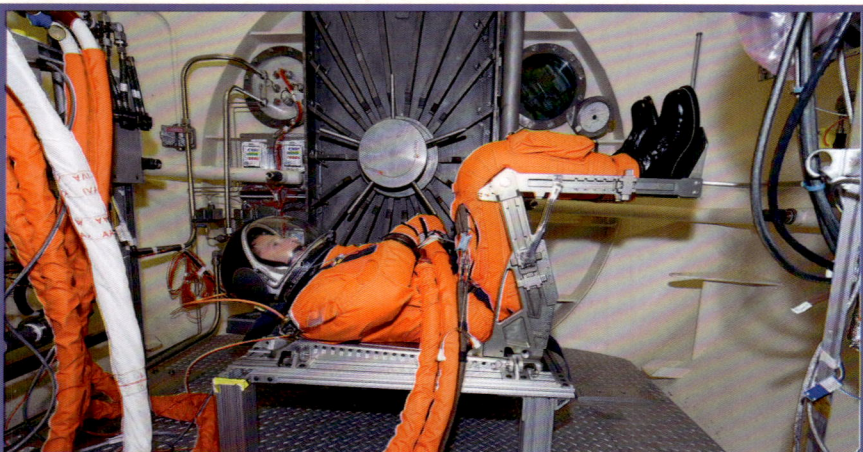

3 PHYSICAL TRAINING

Aspiring astronauts must be in excellent **physical shape**. During training, their bodies are subjected to all kinds of weather tolerance tests and trials. When they are in space, astronauts must do exercise every day.

To acclimatize to their weightlessness, astronauts fly in special planes. When these planes perform drops, they can recreate the sensation of weightlessness for 20 to 25 seconds. This way, astronauts can familiarize themselves with the sensation.

To prepare for spacewalks, the astronauts also train under water. They wear diving equipment and can spend several hours in the pool. The goal of this is to the prepare them for their spacewalks.

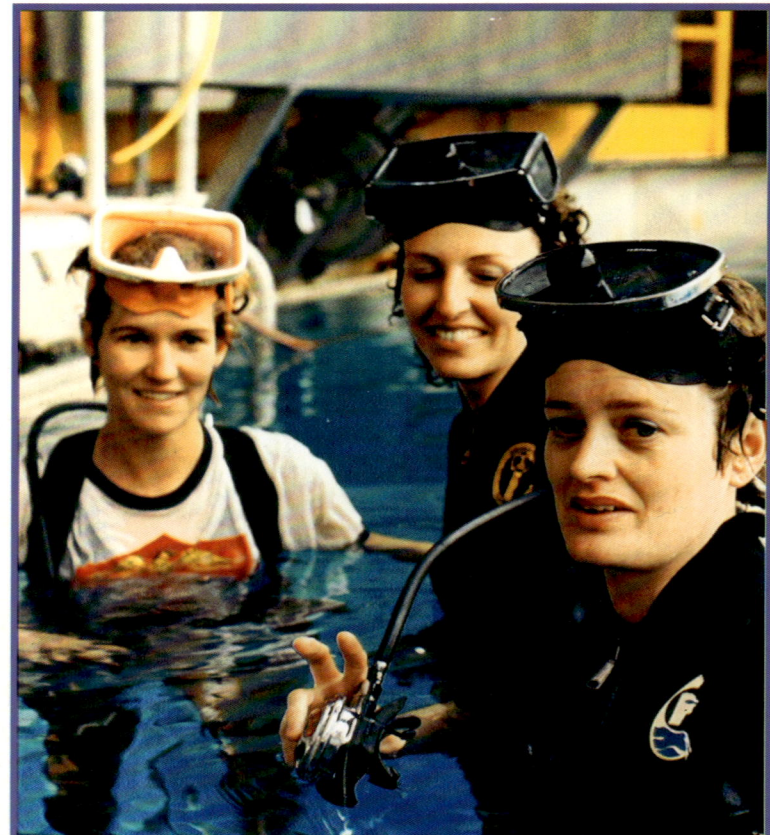

4 MENTAL PREPARATION

Astronauts sometimes face very stressful and unexpected situations. They must know how to keep calm at all times. To prepare, they are put to the challenge under **extreme conditions**.

For example, the CAVES training program is an underground expedition lasting a week developed by the European Space Agency. Participants must work together to carry out complex tasks in **caves that are located 4 km (2.5 mi.) underground**.

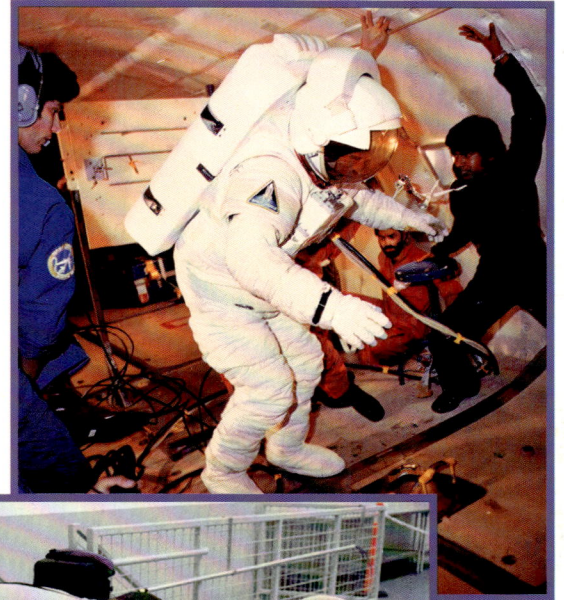

THE SPACE SUIT

Astronauts use different types of space suits to carry out different tasks.

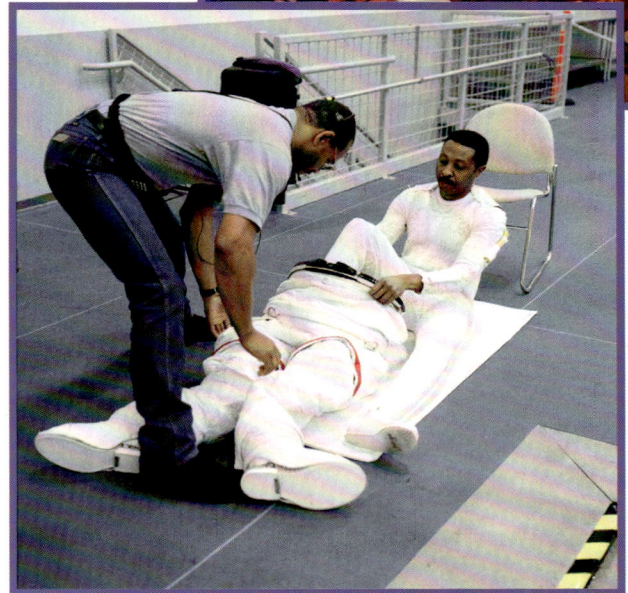

THE ORLAN-M SUIT

It protects the astronauts from **extreme temperatures**, radiation and dusts. It allows the astronauts to act independently for up to 9 hours. The arms and the legs are supple. The helmet and the torso are rigid. They are made of an aluminum alloy. The suit inflates by way of an opening at the back. It is formed of several layers made of different materials. The backpack contains all the essential items necessary for survival and for communication back to Earth. The Orlan-M suit weighs 108 kg (238 lbs.).

53

THE FUTURE OF SPACE EXPLORATION

Oftentimes, in the field of space exploration, reality catches up with science fiction. Nonetheless, space missions keep pushing the frontiers of human knowledge.

THE KEPLER MISSION

Launched in 2009, the *Kepler* spacecraft orbits around the Sun. This giant telescope's mission is to discover planets outside of our solar system. *Kepler* records the rays of light from faraway stars to recognize the passage of planets. We say that a planet is in transit when they pass in front of a star around which it gravitates. To this day, we have identified up to **2500 exoplanets**!

THE REDIRECTION OF AN ASTEROID

In the next decade, NASA will send a robotized spacecraft onto an asteroid. The mission will be to capture a **piece of asteroid** weighing several tons. The spacecraft and the collected rock will be sent into orbit around the Moon. NASA then plans to send astronauts onto it to bring back samples. In preparation for a trip to Mars, NASA will use this mission to test several new technologies.

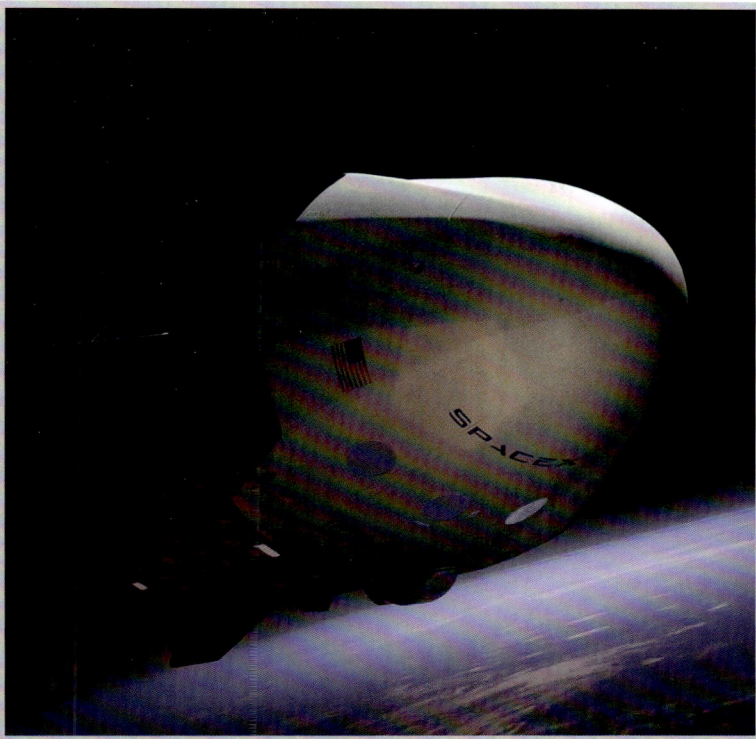

PRIVATE ENTERPRISES

The cost of research and development of new technologies is one of the biggest challenges of space exploration. Governments allot a very small part of their budget to it. This is why space agencies work more and more with private enterprises. The company **SpaceX**, created by Elon Musk, who also launched the electric vehicle Tesla, developed the **first reusable rocket**. SpaceX's spacecrafts are used by NASA to supply the International Space Station.

E.DEORBIT

There are more than **29,000 human-made objects** that orbit around the Earth. A large quantity are debris or inactive satellites. These are dangers and risks to space explorations. Missions from the European Space Agency such as E.Deorbit were launched to clean up a few pieces of this debris.

EUROPA CLIPPER

During its passage near Jupiter, the probe *Galileo* sent back intriguing images of its Moon Europa. We believe that under the frozen surface could be **oceans likely to harbor life**. However, too many questions remain unanswered. The *Europa Clipper* probe will study Jupiter's moon in detail by performing several dozen flights over its surface.

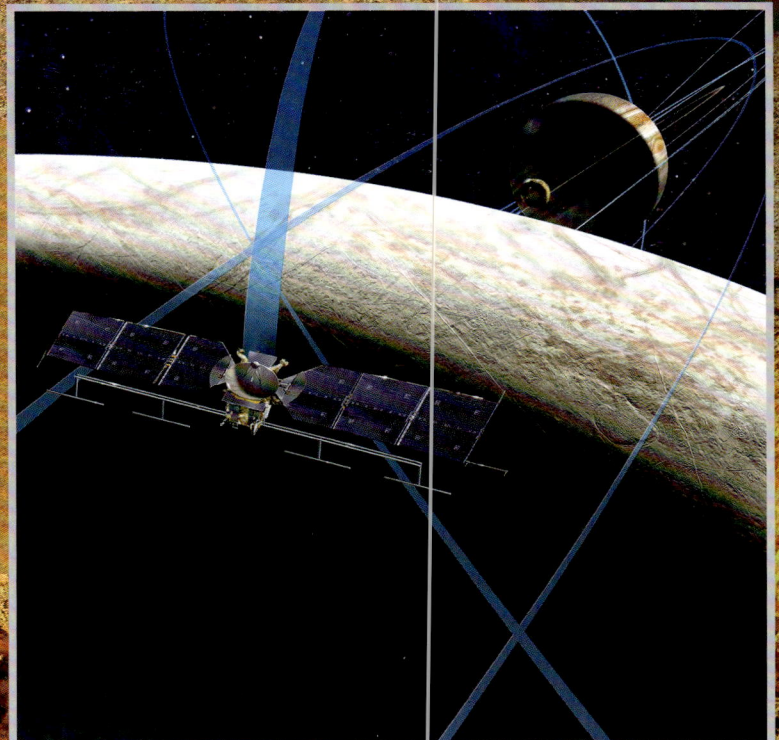

MISSION TO MARS

Even before reaching the Moon, humans have been dreaming about living on Mars. In fact, Space agencies have been preparing for this challenging adventure for several decades. NASA envisions being able to launch the first human missions to Mars by 2030.

The BEAM (Bigelow Expandable Activity Module) is an inflatable module that can serve as housing for crew members on future Mars missions.

GREAT CHALLENGES

With today's technologies, it would take **6 to 9 months** to reach Mars. Missions to the red planet would last at least 3 years. Future explorers of Mars will have to sustain themselves. They will need safe housing, sources of food and sustainable energy. Today's scientists are performing research to surmount many of these obstacles.

To help them, NASA collaborates with schools and American universities. For years, the agency has invited students to propose solutions to several challenges. Many of the innovative concepts are the fruits of their labor.

THE SPACE LAUNCH SYSTEM (SLS) AND THE ORION SPACECRAFT

The new NASA spacecraft are more powerful than ever. The new propulsion systems will allow for explorations to happen further away in space than the lunar orbit.

The new spacecraft *Orion* will also be equipped with a electrical **solar propulsion system**. This technology uses the energy of the Sun to power itself into space. The spacecraft uses 10 times less fuel than current engines.

The SLS and the *Orion* spacecraft combined measure 111 meters (364 feet) in height.

TEST YOUR KNOWLEDGE!

Test the extent of your knowledge on the universe and on space exploration by answering the following questions. If you can't find an answer, try to look back in the book!

THE EARTH

1. **What main material is the air we breathe composed of?**
a) Carbon and nitrogen
b) Mercury and iron
c) Oxygen and nitrogen
d) Helium and nitrogen

2. **What is the function of the ozone layer?**
a) To cool the stratosphere
b) To block the ultraviolet rays of the Sun
c) To prevent asteroids from entering into the atmosphere
d) To block radio waves

3. **In which layer of the atmosphere do airplanes fly?**
a) The thermosphere
b) The stratosphere
c) The troposphere
d) The exosphere

4. **The core of the Earth is formed of:**
a) Carbon and nitrogen
b) Nickel and iron
c) Oxygen and nitrogen
d) Helium and carbon

5. **Earthquakes are caused by:**
a) Tides
b) The movement of tectonic plates
c) The Ozone layer
d) The rays from the Sun

6. **The formation of Earth took place...**
a) 4.6 million years ago
b) 460 years ago
c) 4,600 years ago
d) 4.6 billion years ago

THE MOON

7. **The Moon shines because of:**
a) The rays that it produces
b) The combustible gases its emits
c) The reflection of the rays of the Sun on its surface
d) Space debris

8. **A lunar month lasts approximately:**
a) 12 days
b) 29.5 days
c) 31 days
d) 45 days

9. **The phenomenon of tides is caused by:**
a) The force of attraction between the Moon and the Sun
b) Lunar quakes
c) Waves
d) Storms

OUR SOLAR SYSTEM

10. **After his research, Nicolaus Copernicus affirmed that:**
a) The stars were alive
b) The Earth revolves around the Sun
c) the Sun is a planet
d) the Sun revolves around Earth

11. **The furthest planet from the Sun is:**
a) Earth
b) Mercury
c) Uranus
d) Neptune

12. **All the planets in the solar system except Earth take their name from:**
a) Characters from comic books
b) Undersea regions
c) Greek mythology
d) Chinese astrology

13. The largest planet in our solar system is:

    a) Jupiter

    b) Venus

    c) Uranus

    d) Neptune

14. We say that solar energy is:

    a) Contributable

    b) Renewable

    c) Doubtable

    d) Destructive

15. We now classify Pluto in the category of:

    a) Small planets

    b) Miniscule planets

    c) Magnetic planets

    d) Dwarf planets

THE STARS

16. Stars are born in:

    a) Planets

    b) Nebulae

    c) Hurricanes

    d) Constellations

17. The main sequence of a star is:

    a) The longest phase and the most stable in its life

    b) The moment when the star dies

    c) The quantity of hydrogen that the star contains

    d) The moment of birth

18. What is the name of the celebrated Greek astronomer that indexed 48 constellations in the sky?

    a) Galileo

    b) Ptolemy

    c) Cassiopeia

    d) Perseus

THE GALAXIES

19. What do we call the galaxy in which our solar system is located?

    a) The Andromeda galaxy

    b) Sagittarius

    c) AI 689-xDI

    d) The Milky Way

20. Our solar system is located in the:

    a) Galactic bulb

    b) Great Magellan cloud

    c) Orion belt

    d) Barred spiral

21. What type of galaxy is the Milky Way?

    a) Elliptical

    b) Oval

    c) Rectangular

    d) Barred spiral

SPACE EXPLORATION

22. Neil Armstrong is the first man to:

    a) Be elected president of the United States

    b) Have seen the hidden side of the Moon

    c) Have traveled the Sahara on foot

    d) Have walked on the Moon

23. The International Space Station is equipped with a robotic arm. Who made this arm?

    a) The United States

    b) Russia

    c) The European Union

    d) Canada

24. On what planet do we envision to send the next habitable missions?

    a) Mars

    b) Mercury

    c) Uranus

    d) Neptune

ANSWERS	5. b)	10. b)	15. d)	20. c)
1. c)	6. d)	11. d)	16. b)	21. d)
2. b)	7. c)	12. c)	17. a)	22. d)
3. c)	8. b)	13. a)	18. b)	23. d)
4. b)	9. a)	14. b)	19. d)	24. a)

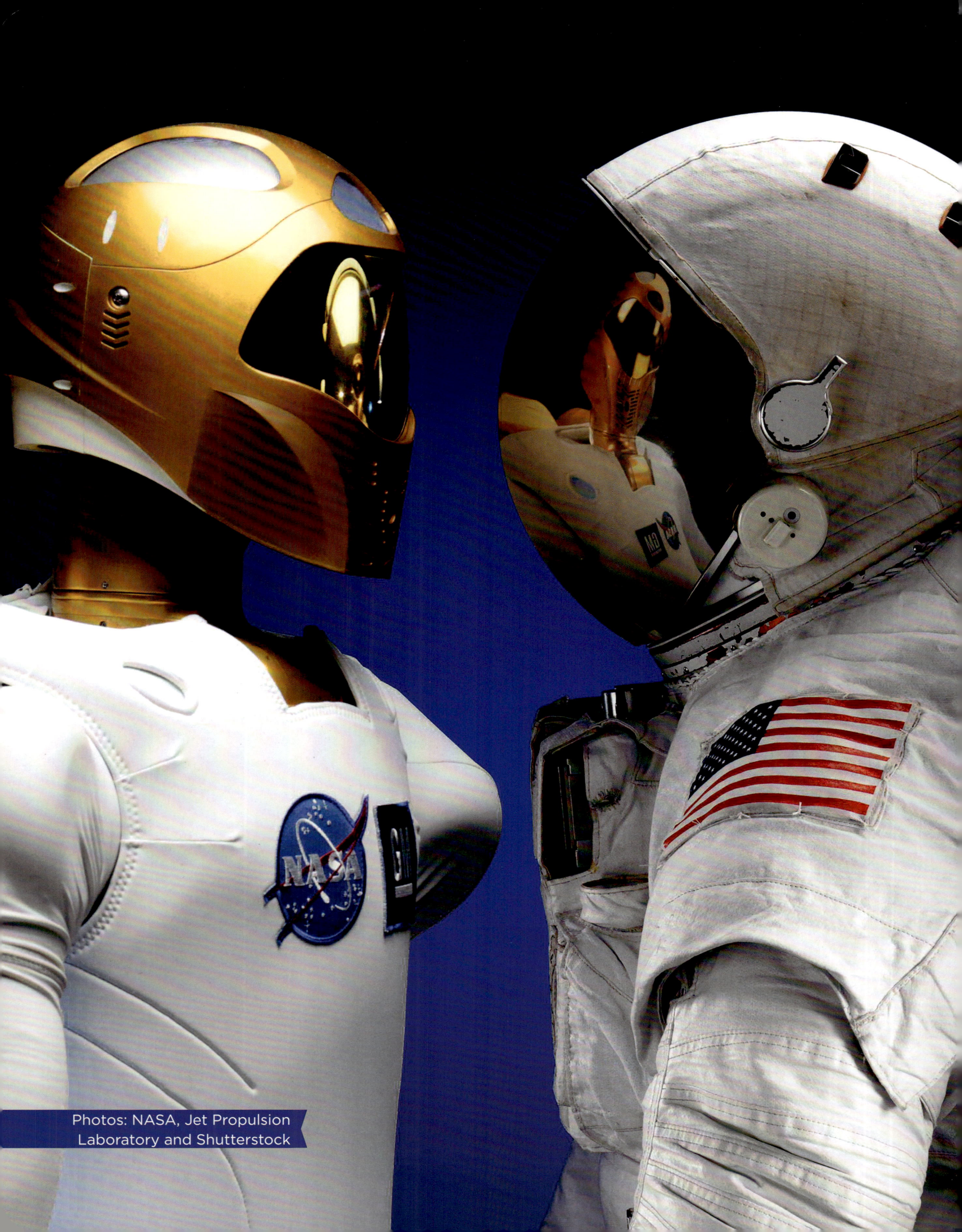